HOW
TO
GET
BIG
RESULTS
FROM A
SMALL
ADVERTISING
BUDGET

HOW
TO
GET
BIG
RESULTS
FROM A
SMALL
ADVERTISING
BUDGET

by Cynthia S. Smith

HAWTHORN BOOKS, INC.
PUBLISHERS / *New York*

To all the little people
who have helped me:
my mother, 5′ 2″,
my father, 5′ 3″,
my daughter Hillary, 5′ 2″,
and big David

CONTENTS

INTRODUCTION
The Psychology of
the Smaller Advertiser

The world of small business is the last frontier of freedom, self-expression, fulfillment, and just plain fun in today's computerized, conglomeratized, commercial arena. It is the only corner left in industry where there is still a concern for people, where an individual can get the opportunity to use every facet of his abilities and to uncover capabilities he never suspected he had.

Handling the advertising of a small or a medium-sized business requires a versatility and multi-view approach that demands some competence in every area of marketing, advertising, and sales promotion and an understanding of the bread-and-butter facts of profitably running a business. There are no crutches such as plans boards, creative committees, and other high-priced personnel group-therapy sessions so favored in the harried halls of large advertising agencies. You are on your own. And in these days of growing remoteness from the results of one's labors, it's downright exhilarating to create something from start to finish and then see the tangible effects firsthand.

This is no place for the one-dimensional individual who can handle only one job at a time, who cannot cope with a mixed bag of responsibilities, who buckles under the confusion of constant interruptions. The ad manager, mar- keting manager, sales promotion manager (whatever title happens to fit on the door of the office assigned), is the resident creative consultant of the small company. To him or her come all questions involving design, style, ad- vertising, taste, public relations, marketing, sales training, sales meetings, trade shows—even what color scheme to use in the executive john.

Unlike the elaborately departmentalized hierarchy of large organizations, the smaller corporate roster is lean, especially in the area of creativity. Common characters in the smaller firm are (1) the president—the tough old bird who started the business and built it up with sweat, faith, and shrewdness; he's the pragmatist who usually doesn't dig design and creativity but is smart enough to recognize the company's need for it; (2) the son (or son-in-law)— also known as the vice-president, whose qualifications for the job are a B.A. and a strong desire to perpetuate the standard of living to which he has become accustomed; (3) the production manager—who runs the factory with an iron hand and whose sense of aesthetics is displayed in the latrine-green and dusty-rose walls he had the truck bays painted. In addition is the usual complement of ac- counting types, sales types, and other people required to perform concrete functions in the company.

Thus as ad manager or ad-agency executive, you are the only individual who works in the area of creativity and intangibles. Since you are also a member of the super- glamorized world known to outsiders as the ad game, you are expected to be familiar with all sorts of exotica. You are the corporate creative arm and must be prepared to be the sole arbiter of all things pertaining to taste, style, color, and design.

It's amazing and amusing to hear the condescension accorded the small-budget advertiser by inhabitants of large agencies. They entertain themselves with the myth that only dropouts from Madison Avenue work in the small-ad field and that any titan of the 4A's could walk into a small company, feed them an economy version of his talents, and score a smasheroo. In actuality, these guys would bomb out in a flash—this has happened over and over again—because handling the advertising of a small business requires a comprehensive array of skills lacking in the usual one-dimensional training of a Madison Avenue laborer. You can't be "just" a copywriter, an artist, etc., who turns over all other tasks to other departments. You must understand market research, media, graphics, direct mail, copywriting, point of purchase, packaging, public relations, TV. You must be able to perform any or all of these jobs or know where and how to buy them.

Incredible as it may seem in this age of the burgeoning of businesses, hundreds of books on advertising are written yearly, and hundreds of advertising courses are given annually, but none addresses itself to the unique demands of small business. They do a great job teaching how to write double-page spreads in *Life*; how to create clever little four-color, six-die-cut brochures; how to produce a cast-of-thousands TV commercial. But how about preparing people to help the tremendous number of small companies who need a series of half-page ads in *Home Furnishings Daily*, or five thousand two-color catalog sheets, or a thirty-second spot TV commercial that cannot cost more than five thousand dollars? These small companies are in dire need of people who are creative, versatile, and realistic—and nowhere is training being offered to meet that need. That's what this book is all about, and that's why it was written. It will give you the basic rudiments of all areas of advertising and sales promotion from the unique point of view of the moderate-budget advertiser. It will show you how to operate effectively within the smaller organization and teach you how to get the most value possible from every dollar of a modest budget.

If you are a principal or executive with a small or a medium-sized company and want to know how to handle your own advertising and sales promotion (or what to expect from the small agency you work with), this book will be of immense help to you.

If you have just graduated from college with advertising training and plan to enter the advertising field but are wise enough to eschew the Doyle, Dane, or die approach to job-hunting, this book will guide you into the tremendously rewarding and exciting field of smaller business.

If you now work in the large agency field and want to get the hell out into the sane, secure world of the smaller advertiser where loyalty and experience are considered assets instead of drawbacks, this book will be of great value to you.

Anyone, anywhere, who wants to get involved in the exhilarating, challenging world of the smaller advertiser, read on—this book is for you.

HOW
TO
GET
BIG
RESULTS
FROM A
SMALL
ADVERTISING
BUDGET

CHAPTER 1

DO-IT-YOURSELF
MARKET RESEARCH

There's a great mystique about market research, promulgated largely, I suspect, by the various organizations who make a handsome living at it. Of course, it's no longer called market research. There's now "motivational research," "behavioral patterns and sciences," and other awe-inspiring euphemisms—all involved in elaborate techniques to elicit information on how to sell products and why and where people will buy them.

Now that's important stuff and of vital interest to anyone preparing to figure out where and how to spend money on advertising and sales promotion. I may scoff at the extremes of specialization in the areas of market research, at the heavy stress on libido and id and consumer psychoanalysis, but that's what makes news for the clients as well as for the service purveyors.

But a small company is not out to make news—just sales. And there's a basic framework of whys, wheres, and hows that must be constructed before you can build any sort of promotional and marketing program. It's particularly difficult to amass this basic data in a small company. The kind of market-analysis information that is lying around in large companies, just waiting to be tapped, is often totally absent in small organizations, where executives are long on gut reactions and short on facts. For instance, you'll frequently find that management has no statistics on regional sales of each product; they may know that a particular item sells well, but they don't know where it sells better or if it moves faster in certain areas at specific times.

This is why, by the way, the big-league-trained ad person finds it hard to apply his talents to smaller companies: In the little leagues you can take nothing for granted. If you need information, you dig it out yourself.

DETERMINING THE MARKETING STRUCTURE

Okay, let's begin. You want to uncover the full picture of the company's existing marketing situation. Before you can move into planning, you must be fully aware of its weaknesses and strengths. In the absence of computerized data, I have evolved a very simple method of eliciting the basic facts. It's not as scientific as one might like, but over the years it has proved surprisingly exact. It's called interrogating the boss.

The term "boss" is a loosely applied one. It's the person in charge—usually the one who founded the firm or built it up to its present position. His or her head contains most of the data you need, but it takes judicious questioning and interpreting to sift out the accurate information. (If *you* are the boss, it will be slightly tougher, but try to be objective.)

Beware of the following pitfalls. Remember that this individual's opinions are often based on judgments made when he or she was last out in the field—which could be twenty years ago. So listen for the facts, and ignore the judgments. Remember, too, that he or she has been so wrapped up in the company that his vision is frequently clouded by proprietary feelings that tend to cloud his objectivity. For example, he will undoubtedly refer to his company as pioneers or leaders in the industry. I have yet to encounter a small-company president who did not state this conviction with great emphasis and pride. Never mind that. I figure that anyone who has succeeded in the onerous task of building a company is entitled to that conceit; he's earned it. But I do mind when they express a deep conviction that their customers really care. It's often hard to convince them that nobody really gives much of a damn what your company contributed to the industry fifteen years ago—or fifteen hours ago, for that matter. Customers deal with nows, and so must we.

Now that you are fully prepared for the pitfalls, have the boss sit down, arm yourself with pen and pad, and ask away.

In which market are company products now being sold?

Possible answers might be in terms of economic categories (such as, if you have an art gallery, and most of your paintings are bought by persons making fifty thousand dollars a year and over, whereas lithographs and prints are going primarily to those making twenty thousand a year and under). They might be in terms of professions (such as, if you are an insurance broker, and you find that higher-cost annuity policies are being bought primarily by doctors, whereas straight life policies are preferred by lawyers). There could be trade markets (such as, if you are a pencil-manufacturer or a distributor of specialized types of pencils that go to architects, artists, accountants).

There could be ethnic markets (such as, if you sell books on investment and you find that the largest groups of purchasers are Orientals and Jews).

In which other markets do you think these products could be sold?

Here you can come up with some imaginative lulus. But take note, and distill practical reality from unrealistic thinking. Beware of the situation like that of the manufacturer who put one of his small industrial soda fountains (which retailed for only five thousand dollars) in his playroom bar and believed that there was a large potential market for it for home use. There's a thread of an idea here, but you certainly couldn't accept his forecast for a mass-market potential without doing a lot of further investigation.

What are the current methods of distribution?

Company salesmen: These are people employed solely by the company and paid directly by them. This is the best setup from a sales-promotional point of view, because company salesmen are the most cooperative and responsive. They have to be—their jobs depend on it. They can be counted on to distribute advertising material, to follow up sales leads, to see that counter and window displays are set up when and where you want.

Manufacturer's representatives: This is usually an organization of two or more individuals who represent many companies in an allied field. They are independent agents who sell the products of a number of companies, usually of a related category that can be sold to the same outlets. They are paid commission for what they sell. The company handles billing and shipping.

Representatives are harder to handle and present more of a challenge to creators of sales-promotional material. For one thing, they are independent entrepreneurs, and although your company's line is important to them, they are not totally dependent—it is just one of many. This means you won't be able to issue orders or make heavy demands on their time. Their sales technique involves a quick hit and run in each outlet they call on. In the maybe ten minutes' time the buyer allots them they must show and sell perhaps a dozen different products. So they are not likely to want to use any of that valuable time for any nonselling activity, such as setting up displays or talking up advertising campaigns. Also, they will not carry any cumbersome material. If you have ever gone around with any of these salesmen and watched them lug in cases of samples and selling literature, you would appreciate their reluctance to add further burdens.

So when you find that you are dealing with a manufacturer's rep situation, be aware of the natural limitations, and prepare your material accordingly.

Wholesale distributors: These are companies who buy merchandise from many firms and resell it to small outlets. They are, in effect, middlemen, who stock, ship, and bill and who employ their own salesmen.

This method of distribution means the least amount of advertising cooperation. It means that the ultimate seller of your products has no contact with your company; he deals only with the wholesaler. And the wholesaler's salesman has no loyalty to you at all—his salary comes from the wholesaler.

Is the company satisfied with its sales in each territory?
You will undoubtedly learn that some areas are weaker in sales than others. It is vital that you analyze why. There are two common answers: lousy salesmen and lousy territory.

Lousy salesmen: You will be told that slow sales in a specific area are due to the ineptness of the local salesmen. That may or may not be true. It's important that you check this out; the results will determine areas of advertising expenditure. Find out if other salesmen who previously covered that territory fared better, under the same conditions. If he is a manufacturer's rep who sells other companies' products, does he perform equally poorly for them? If you have, in fact, a rotten sales force in the area and it cannot be replaced readily, you will have to plan some hard-hitting local campaigns to help it along.

Lousy territory: The other standard complaint—that one territory is particularly difficult—may have some validity. If you're selling boating supplies, you can't expect too heavy a volume in Tucson, Arizona. If you're selling gold jewelry, you won't anticipate too wild a response in Bobtown, Pennsylvania.

What you have to watch for here are *excuses* instead of reasons. After a while you can develop the ability to detect what psychiatrists call the emotional sound. You will hear the false ring of an excuse. Here are two of the oldest sales-failure bromides of them all: "They only buy from buddies down there." The gist of this theory is that a fierce regional loyalty exists in the area and that only local boys can make good there. Nonsense. I've heard this one over and over again and found it phony every time. True, a customer may prefer to buy from a buddy, but business is business. Give a buyer a profit-making product or an item that pleases him or her more than someone else's, and he'll buy yours over his brother's. Money creates a unique selfishness; the desire to get the best for the money transcends all emotional considerations.

"Competition has the area all sewed up." This may or may not be so. But before you accept it as gospel, be aware that businessmen usually have an overblown image of how well their competitors are doing. This reasoning is usually a compound of jealousy, plus the assumption that "if we're not getting the business, someone else must." Sometimes, however, no one has really tapped the full potential of an area. The only way to find the real facts is to pay a visit to the area. See as many buyers as you can. Ask questions, and look around; you may find the most amazing reasons for sluggish sales.

I was once assured by a manufacturer's representative that the entire city of Cleveland was off limits for our line of products because, whereas he was based in Chicago and could get to Cleveland only a few times a year, the competitor had a resident salesman in the city. How could he compete with a salesman who dropped in on the dealers every week?

I went out there to look the situation over. And I found out that in one respect he was right: The competitor did have a resident salesman in Cleveland, an elderly semiretired gentleman who had little to do, handled just the one line, and enjoyed visiting the dealers often. But I also discovered that the storekeepers did not take pleasure in his frequent visits. They found him a pain in the neck who demanded too much of their valuable time. Even more important, I noticed that although they did buy all of that category of merchandise from the competitor, all that they bought was not nearly enough for a city like Cleveland. There was very little on the shelves, and none displayed. Obviously there was some weakness in the selling presentation.

Just a little questioning of the buyers, the sales clerks, and the store-managers quickly indicated the low importance they assigned to the entire product category. Obviously they considered it a minor line with limited appeal.

The situation was quite simple to remedy. All that had to be done was to mount a city-wide sales-promotion and advertising campaign. The promotion produced a volume of demand that the dealers never knew existed. It showed that they had been overlooking a valuable source of sales —a situation they were most eager to rectify, of course. From that point on, they began to buy the whole line in depth unprecedented for Cleveland, featuring it on counters and in windows—and selling. Another important side benefit was the attitude of our company's manufacturer's representative. He learned that he could indeed sell in a city he had long since given up. The experience taught him never to yield a territory under those conditions again.

AFTER INTERROGATING THE BOSS

Now that you have picked the boss's brain clean, it's time to move on to another ranking member of the firm, with the same bank of questions. It might be the sales manager, general manager, sometimes even the head bookkeeper. In small companies you frequently run into situations where an unspecified individual with no discernible title turns out to be the one who really runs the joint. It's easy to identify this person. When you are questioning the boss, if more than three times he counters your question with "Wait, I'll ask Charlie," then you know that Charlie's your man. Get to him next, and ask him exactly the same questions you have asked his employer. It is vital to have his more objective, less emotional point of view as a backup check to the facts you have already accumulated.

Incidentally, this do-it-yourself market-research probe can have beneficial side effects for you personally. You will find that you have made a very solid impression upon management. And if you're new with the company, it will send you off to an auspicious start.

Remember that a good question reveals the insight and acumen of the questioner as well as the questioned. You will notice that people enjoy answering these sorts of questions. First, they are basically flattered that you want to consult them and value their opinions. Second, it gives them an opportunity to expand their minds and make them aware of knowledge they may not have known they possessed. The boss will enjoy discussing his accomplishments and will feel that you have a true understanding of his problems.

Now that you have accumulated all the information, you

have a picture of how, where, and what the company sells. You are prepared to plan a marketing strategy that will be aimed at remedying the weaknesses and exploiting the strengths you have discovered.

WHERE TO PICK UP VALUABLE MARKETING FACTS

Trade Publications

Every industry has its share of trade publications. It's their business to have statistics on the buying and selling habits of the industry. And this valuable information is yours for the asking. For instance, they can usually supply you with a listing of the peak selling months in your industry, plus a geographic breakdown of the largest consumption areas in the country.

Think of how invaluable that can be. Suppose your questioning has turned up the fact that sales in the Southwest dropped last year. Then the trade publication's survey figures show that area's sales to have enjoyed a remarkable general upsurge last year, possibly due to new industry or new marketing awareness in the territory. Obviously something is very wrong in your sales department.

Or perhaps you learn that most people in the industry do very poorly in summer, and your company does fantastically well in those months. Such a disparity rings an alarm bell. Find out what you are doing right. Perhaps you are doing something different in June, July, and August. Check. You may discover a sales technique that you can apply successfully the rest of the year. You can learn a great deal from successes as well as from failures.

A great source for general sales information is the magazine *Sales Management.* It contains all sorts of facts and figures about the national marketing picture that you could find extremely useful.

The most important thing about trade publications is their desire to actively help companies in their industry. I have great faith in altruism. But there's nothing like the profit motive to get guys off their butts to give you immediate action. True, there's a lot of information you can pick up from government pamphlets. But did you ever try to get fast action from a government employee?

If you want to break into a new field and want to set up a sales force, the trade-publication space salesman will gladly help you do so. He knows that once you prepare to introduce your products to a new field, you will want to advertise to reach the potential buyers. And that will mean advertising billing for him. It's a very open relationship—one hand washing the other, and all that. You don't have to make any false promises or commitments. Any space salesman worth his salt knows he must invest a certain amount of his time in cultivating potential customers, and he'll give you all the marketing and promotional help he can.

The publications usually have a list of all the salesmen and manufacturer's sales representatives and wholesale distributors in the industry. They also usually know who's good, who's eager, who's looking for new lines, and will gladly steer you to the right sales organization.

Take advantage of the services and cooperation offered by the trade publications; it can be invaluable.

Read your trade publications carefully. You will find a wealth of information in them. Clip and collect competitors' ads and publicity as well as your own. Develop a "swipe file" (more properly called a reference file); it's always handy to know what everyone else is doing.

Company Salesmen

Salesmen are the central intelligence banks of the business world. Treat them with consideration and loving care, and you'll turn up the hottest market-research information you can hope for.

You realize that these men are out in the market, in the field, in the battle lines every day. They are continually in contact with the buyers and the buying public. The only thing you must also realize is that few of them are at all aware of the valuable information they carry. It's up to you to pry it loose.

It's not hard. They respond eagerly to simple consideration and attentiveness. You must understand that these men are out all day taking guff, rudeness, and rebuffs. Then they come back to the home office and are bawled out for not selling enough or not checking properly on someone's credit. Or they learn that the order they sweated over for two months, nurturing a customer to develop him into an account, cannot be shipped for another four weeks. They are loaded with gripes, and there's no place to unburden them. Let your office become the unburdening depot, and you'll turn up a wealth of goodies as well as make life easier for these heroic men of the road.

What sort of things can you learn? You can discover new and unusual uses for your company's products and what kind of displays are needed at the point of purchase. All sorts of ideas come out when you give salesmen a chance to talk to you about their experiences.

A good way to get them started is to mention the specific success of another salesman. Salesmen by nature are garrulous and somewhat egoistical, and someone else's success always prods them. For instance, you might open with "I hear Dave Johnson is selling that little machine light to sewing-machine manufacturers by the thousands.

Great idea, isn't it?" Inevitably, he'll come up with a parallel unusual application that he uncovered—some sale he has made that could open an entirely new marketing outlet.

Minds run in odd ways and need different sorts of stimuli. If you had asked him the direct question "Have you uncovered any unusual uses for this light?" he would undoubtedly have racked his brain for a moment and then come up empty. That's a thing to remember in all your do-it-yourself market research. *Never ask a direct question that invites a "yes" or "no" answer.* People are too ready to take the lazy way out and say No. Appeal to their egos, and you'll get action.

I once uncovered a gold mine by asking a salesman why he sold so few of the company's credit-card cases and wallet inserts. Stung to the quick by my casting aspersions on his selling ability, he came up with a quick answer that revolutionalized and quadrupled the company's sales of that group of products: "Because it takes too damn long to sell all those little penny-ante plastic cases. It's nickel-and-dime stuff, and by the time the customer picks out which styles he wants, I've spent ten minutes, and I end up with a lousy six-dollar sale. Now if you had a whole prepacked assortment that I could say, 'Look, fella, this is it—it's got all the best items in the line,' I could maybe sell him forty dollars worth of stuff in half the time!"

It was, of course, a great idea, and we all wondered why no one had ever thought of it before. But then, that's usually the way with the most obviously simple things, isn't it? A counter display of the ten most popular cases was created and retailed for $46.50. Not only did it make the initial order far easier, but subsequent orders took no time at all. The salesmen just went in and checked the inventory and wrote orders for whatever replacement merchandise was required.

Space Salesmen

Advertising salesmen for the trade magazines are people of real importance. More than anyone else, they know what's going on in the field—the gossip, the facts, the rumors, the scuttlebutt. You'll find out where and when your competitors advertise and what markets they plan to enter. If you are looking for a job, by the way, or some key company personnel to fill a vacancy or new accounts if you have an advertising agency, these are the boys who can help. Just be friendly and hospitable, and keep your ears open. You'll soon find out who's doing what to whom and for how much and a pack of data that might come in handy.

Order Clerks

The company order clerk—anyone who takes orders over the phone or processes the incoming written orders —is another local treasure of market data. Order clerks are aware of the ultimate destination of the company's products, since they see the shipping addresses on the orders. This can alert you to entirely new markets.

Ask them to advise you when they come across something out of the ordinary—an unusual destination, a type of company they are not accustomed to dealing with, an exotic locality they are not used to seeing. Ask every order clerk, "Have you come across any unusual uses for our products today?" They will be most cooperative. The day of an order clerk can be mighty dreary. Any bit of creative spice you can impart is much appreciated. Also, it gives them a feeling of importance and involvement with the company's advertising program.

Just as an illustration of the sort of valuable information you can turn up in this way, I'll take you back to that manufacturer of soda-fountain equipment and that small soda-fountain unit he had installed in his home.

An alert order clerk began to notice that one salesman was selling a number of these small units to hospitals, an unusual destination for this type of equipment. She advised us, and we contacted the salesman to learn his secret. It was a beaut. It seems that every hospital has a large number of restricted-diet patients on each floor who are not permitted the usual sugared soft drinks. The smart salesman sold hospitals on the idea of putting a small soda-fountain unit of sugar-free sodas on each floor where the nurse could draw drinks conveniently.

This little tip led to a whole advertising campaign to hospitals and the ultimate sale of thousands of dollars' worth of these units.

TESTING A NEW PRODUCT

Someone in the company has come up with what looks like a great idea for a product. Everyone thinks it has potential. But how can you be sure, before you plunk thousands into production, that it will sell? And further, how do you know which aspects of the new product are the most appealing to the buying public?

In other words, is there a big need for it to justify the investment? And if so, what will be the prime motivation for someone to buy it? Here's what you do to get the answers to these million-dollar questions with a minimum of expenditure.

Focus group interviewing is the technique used by million-dollar concerns and advertising agencies and is easily adaptable to small budgets. It involves assembling cross-section groups and getting their reactions to the product. Here's how to go about it.

Type of group: Be selective but random about whom you gather. If you are testing a consumer product, be sure you have people who will be in the proper purchasing power group for that item. In other words, don't question Fifth Avenue matrons about men's work clothes. If it's a product that will be bought by both men and women, have representatives of both sexes. Ascertain that you are in the right age group, too. Don't have teeny-boppers in the group when you are evaluating denture cream.

Size of group: From eight to ten is the right size. Too much bigger gets unwieldy and loses the intimacy that leads to the exchange of ideas you seek. Fewer won't tell you enough.

Method—how to proceed: Assemble the group in a proper-sized room—not a gigantic hall that makes everyone feel uncomfortable and uneasy. The keynote must be ease and informality. Serve them coffee to foster relaxation. Then start with a little talk thanking them for coming and stating how you value their judgments and are eager to have their opinions.

Then demonstrate the product. If it's a food, pass it around and let them taste it, see it, and touch it. Then start with your questions. They must be carefully structured to suggest nothing—merely to elicit reaction.

For instance, if you want to know how they like the look of a product, don't ask a straight like-it-or-not question. The result is useless. Too many people will say Yes because they hate to hurt your feelings, and many will say No because they enjoy being provocative.

Sneak in the back way with a gambit like "Which room would you place this table in?" If it ends up that they can't see the piece in any room, then you know you've got a redesigning problem on your hands.

If you want to know what price range the product should fall into, don't ask, "How much would you be willing to pay for this?" Suggest a few prices, and see which range they consider feasible.

You must be extremely attentive at all times and be sure

to guide the group to prevent any dominant types from taking over. This is one of the dangers of any group session; there's always the bigmouth who loves to hog the floor and the shyer ones who are afraid to speak up. You must watch for this. Steer away from the extroverts, and draw out the quiet ones with questions to bring them into the discussion.

Keep on the alert for new ideas, too. Sometimes a suggestion for a new application for the product crops up. Pick up the lead, and get everyone's opinion on the potential.

Find out what colors they prefer, where they would expect to buy it, for whom in the family they would buy it.

One or two of these sessions, and you will have a pretty fair idea of the dominant marketing theme that should be stressed, what price range the product must fall into, and whether or not it has sufficient potential to bring it in at all.

TEST PROMOTION CAMPAIGN

Now the product is ready to go. To insure your investment even more, the next step is to prepare and run a test ad campaign in one area.

There are accepted favorite test cities in the United States which are used all the time. These are: Albany, Columbus, Denver, Des Moines, Fort Wayne, Grand Rapids, Hartford, Indianapolis, Minneapolis, Omaha, Phoenix, Providence, Rochester, and Syracuse. These cities have passed the test for testing. They have apparently proved to be cross sections that are the closest to the national norm. But your choice must be governed by other factors as well, because you have a cost factor to consider.

You must select the test city that is closest to the home

office, so that the costs of materials, manpower, and shipping will be lowest, and so that the city will be covered by the kind of cooperative, promotion-minded salesmen you need. It is imperative that you work with active, efficient salesmen for a test campaign.

Now prepare a small test run of all the promotion material you plan to use: circulars, ads, window streamers, displays. If you can afford TV—great; local TV time can sometimes be bought reasonably, and don't overlook radio.

Pack it all into one concentrated week during the buying season for the product you are introducing (no ski boots in July, etc.). Then be sure that there's no local event that will fall within that week and detract from your campaign, no national holiday that might close stores, schools, and offices or in some way alter the shopping patterns unfavorably.

Send your salesmen around at least a month before to line up participation, to interest stores in cooperative advertising tie-ins, to arrange for store and window displays, and to be sure that every possible store has merchandise to back up the promotion. Last but not least, check with your own main offices to be sure that the merchandise is on hand ready to be shipped and in the stores in advance.

Then you get up there and see what kind of publicity tie-ins with local papers and radio stations you can get.

Pour all your ammunition into that week. The effect will be a full-scale assault that will make every potential buyer in the city aware of the product. *And be there yourself.* Move around, get to the stores; hear what the salesclerks say, what the customers say. See that the displays keep stocked.

By the end of the week you will know pretty much how good the product is and how effective the advertising promotion is. You will have all the information you need to make your marketing decisions about the product.

This campaign may cost a bit of a bundle, but it is a very small investment compared to what you can be stuck with if the product turns out to be a bomb. Remember the Edsel.

CHAPTER 2

MEDIA SELECTION

The word "budget" usually connotes caution with cash and limited income. But in my experience "advertising budgets" exist strictly in the province of big-money land. The little fellow's advertising expenditures are usually handled in a freewheeling way that would horrify the structured scientific soul of a Harvard Business School type. In the impulsive play-it-by-ear world of small business the "advertising budget" is just a series of figures compiled at the beginning of each year to make everyone feel that correct modern business methods are being observed.

"Work up a recommended advertising program for the year," the ad agency is told. And after much research, selective readership statistics, and arithmetic, the agency comes up with a conscientious schedule of where and how the moneys should be allocated. It is impressively typed in triplicate and then distributed at a meeting consisting of the agency and all important, interested client personnel. There, amid a great deal of heated discussion of the budget, followed by judicious evaluation and cautious consolidation (translation: nit-picking and hacking away), the annual advertising program is set. And everyone exits in a flurry of good fellowship and the satisfaction of a job well done.

Then the next day the arch competitor comes out with a knock-off of the company's chief product, and the whole program is obliterated as the company president hollers for immediate ads and direct-mail promotions to counteract this gross indignity.

In small business nothing is permanent and irrevocable. You have to meet special situations as they arise. It is this ability to be flexible that gives the smaller business a big advantage over big business. You can work fast and hit fast without being forced to await decisions and approvals from conglomerated committees.

Still, you should arrive at a budget—some idea of how much the company can spend on advertising for the coming year and where you think it should go. Even though you all know that it can be altered, it's a framework to work with and gives a certain amount of direction to the total promotional effort.

THE VALUE OF TRADE MAGAZINES

Every business has its trade publications. They are the life force of an industry. Every individual who is in any way involved in that industry reads the trade publications, since they are the prime sources of news and educational information that he must have in order to function efficiently. If you want to know what everyone is doing and where and how, it's in the trade publication. And if you want others to know what you are doing, you must advertise in the trade publication. There are many ways and reasons to use trade advertising.

Institutional Advertising

I hate to mention "institutional" because the word is usually an anathema to pragmatic, hard-nosed business-men. Naturally.

Institutional advertising is the sort of ads that say: "Hello, everybody, here we are. This is our name, and this is what we do." It doesn't really sell anything other than image. To the small businessman this is a luxury he usually feels he cannot afford. He likes to see every buck spent produce a tangible result—like a sales lead or a sale. Institutional ads don't produce inquiries; they don't produce immediate sales. But they are necessary to achieve some very important effects and to solve some very serious problems.

Take our client who suddenly enjoyed tremendous growth. Since production facilities had not yet caught up with the new sales figures, they were behind in deliveries and behind in correspondence. While they were working feverishly on expansion plans to accommodate this new activity, the competition took advantage of their chaos to whisper around that the company was bordering on bankruptcy. When these rumors started to become danger-ous, it was important to run institutional advertising to let the industry know that they were still in business. A series of ads appeared in all the trade publications that made it quite apparent that the company was very much alive and kicking.

Prestige Buildup

"Prestige"—that elusive word that contributes so con-cretely to growth. The subliminal effect of seeing a name repeatedly has the effect of attaching the name to that class of product.

Of course, it took millions to develop the association

of the name "Kleenex" with tissues and "Frigidaire" with refrigerators. But on a smaller scale that sort of status is what can be achieved by consistent advertising in the trade media.

Buying-Time Reminders

Direct mail acts immediately or not at all. It directs the recipient to take a specific action *now* and then toss the piece away. It's not meant to leave a lasting impression; direct mail is a one-shot deal. But ads are there, in front of the buyers for a day, a week, a month. And every time they go through the publication, your ad registers and builds up a subconscious reminder factor that clicks into action when ordering time comes around.

Opening Doors for Salesmen

It's bad enough when your salesman walks into a new prospect and says, "Hello, I'm Charlie Rollins."

And the buyer says, "Charlie who?"

But it's worse when the salesman comes back with, "You know, Charlie Rollins, from Tooth and Nail Medical Supply Company."

And the prospect says, "The Tooth and what company?"

Then your man is in trouble. And it's your fault.

Trade advertising makes the company name instantly familiar to prospects and opens doors for salesmen. It assures a warmer reception on cold calls, when they need all the help they can get. And it keeps the doors open and makes their jobs easier.

I've heard small businessmen say proudly, "We don't need trade advertising. Everyone in the business knows us." Sure—maybe last year, last month, or last week. But new buyers come into a field every day; new businesses open every week. If you don't keep your name around constantly, where everyone can see it, it will be as quickly forgotten as last year's Miss America.

Introducing a New Product

When you are bringing out a new product or launching a special promotion, trade advertising must be the hub of it. Your big announcement should hit the pages of the trade pubs and be coordinated with all other elements of the promotion.

Preparing a Reception for Your Direct Mail

You would hesitate to buy a TV set from a street peddler. Who knows what's inside the cabinet, and where do you go for service? So how can you expect anyone to buy your products from a cold direct-mail solicitation if they don't know who you are?

A mailing comes out of nowhere. It's an impersonal piece of paper that is dropped on a desk by a usually faceless postman. It has no connection to a real, live company unless you build one. Trade-paper advertising builds your image as a substantial, reliable known quantity. They know your name; they know you are a solid organization and not some hole-in-the-wall operation. And when your mailing hits their desks, they recognize, read, and respond. Trade advertising establishes your position and thus increases the effectiveness of your direct mail.

WHICH TRADE PUBLICATIONS TO PICK

First, see if you can get your hands on a *Standard Rate & Data, Business Publications* issue (the green volume) and also the *Consumer Magazine* issue (the orange volume). These are the bibles of the media buyer. They list all publications according to industry or category and give rates, circulation, and every kind of information you need. You must be a subscriber to get copies, and every advertising agency is. Ask your friendly neighborhood ad agency to give you back copies. They are issued every few months, and the oldies only get thrown out anyway.

Now call or write each magazine in your industry and ask (1) for copies of their three latest issues and (2) to have a space salesman call. But before you see the salesman, carefully read and analyze each magazine yourself.

Design and appearance: Does it look well printed, well-designed? Now don't say, "What do I know? I'm not an art critic," because there's a great deal you can tell by instinctive response to a magazine. You may not be able to define your reaction, but you can rely here on that old bromide "I don't know anything about art; I just know what I like." A poorly printed publication—and I've seen some lulus that looked as if they'd been run off on a hand-press for distribution at smoker movies—will have smeared, gray-looking type, fuzzy pictures, and cruddy paper. If it's poorly designed (maybe too few pictures, too heavy concentration of type), it will not invite readership. If it looks cheap and sleazy, it will make your company look cheap and sleazy, so skip it.

How much advertising does it carry? This is a good clue to a publication's effectiveness as a selling medium. If it carries just a desultory scattering of ads, then it is wanting in some department, because if it were a valuable publication that reached and affected buyers, the ad-agency media people would have put their clients' money into it. If they bypassed it, so should you.

Of course, that's not a hard and fast rule. When a magazine is new, it might not yet have picked up advertising momentum but still have a very high rate of readership. And be sure you look through a few issues so that you are not misled by seasonal slumps. Summer issues carry a relatively light advertising load.

Whose advertising does it carry? Notice the quality of the ads and the companies represented. If the book seems filled with poor-put-together ads (of companies you never even heard of), they are probably pub-set. That means the publication's usually minimal art facility has produced the ad free for a company who could not afford ad-agency services. At the risk of sounding like a snob, if it doesn't attract better advertisers than that, it isn't much of a publication.

Does the publication appeal to your specific segment of the market? Most fields have many facets, and each trade magazine develops its own sort of constituency. You want to be sure that you're going in the magazine that reaches your part of the market. For example, in the interior-design field there are two market categories— traditional and contemporary. And there are two major publications in the field. If you look through the magazines, you will notice that the editorial content and merchandise advertised in one is heavily traditional, with a token contemporary section. The other book is filled with almost exclusively contemporary furnishings. In the stationery field there are social stationers and commercial stationers. One magazine is basically commercial, with a section devoted to greeting cards and sundry social-stationery merchandise. Another publication is weighted the other way around.

You select the publication that is slanted predominantly toward your specific area. If it has merely a section devoted to your interest, that means it reaches just a section of the market. Why pay full price for an ad that reaches only a fraction of your market?

HOW TO LISTEN TO SPACE SALESMEN

These eager gentlemen, the space salesmen, are some of the best-trained, best-informed, and best-equipped salespeople you will ever encounter. They will present you with enough charts, graphs, readership studies, and attaché-case-loads of facts and figures to make the mind boggle.

Listen to them. And then ask your questions.

But watch out for alibi words that indicate poor circulation, like "secondary pass-along circulation." That means they are trying to claim that their publication not only is read by a subscriber, but is passed on to the crowd of ardent fans who are milling around his desk just awaiting their turn at the magazine. Since this readership claim cannot be measured, if it indeed exists, forget it. It is usually the weak statement of a weak publication.

I've heard all kinds of circulation allegations by some overzealous underequipped space salesmen. Like the fellow who told me that his magazine had the "highest restroom circulation"—that you find it in more dealer toilets than any other publication in the industry. You realize, of course, that you would then be enjoying a sort of captive readership, a unique situation that assures intensive perusal of the publication. To my knowledge no statistical organization has yet chosen to compile and evaluate these alleged facts and figures. You know that any space salesman touting this sort of data has to have a lousy book. All you want to know about is proved, audited circulation.

DIRECT RESPONSE—THE HOT NEW MEDIUM

"Direct response" is a whole new breed of cat which has arisen in the last few years. It had existed in a few fields but has proliferated to the point that the category now has its own special section in *Standard Rate & Data*—an accolade of advertising trade recognition tantamount to being invited to join the United Nations.

In effect, it's actually a hybrid: a cross between direct mail and a trade publication. It is a collection of product postcards, bound together in booklet form. Each advertiser has a single card, arranged in standard format, with the product on front and a return address on back. The interested reader merely detaches the card and mails it in. It's easy and immediate.

This medium works very much like direct mail, with a few differences—some good, some bad. On the plus side you get mailed to a huge interested list without paying the mammoth postage and handling costs all by yourself. You travel with a good crowd. The collection of cards has the substantial effect of a buying source guide and is likely to be held on to far longer than would a single piece of direct mail. On the negative side you can show only one product or service on a card and are restricted to a very limiting format.

The direct-response medium can pull a tremendous volume of inquiries. Many of my students have reported success stories that resulted not only in large numbers of inquiries, but in a high percentage of actual sales.

If you are looking for inquiries, if you have a sales organization that is dependent on your referrals, this is a sure way to get them.

WHERE TO PUT YOUR MONEY

In the final analysis which trade publication do you put your money on? After you have heard all the pitches and analyzed all the publications, it's often still hard to decide where to go.

If your budget can stand it, go in all of them—that is, all the publications that reach your market and are reliable books. There are usually at least two of the category in each field. I suggest that you hit all of them because the trade publications are important to you. Their goodwill is a handy thing to have, and you can get help from them that is available nowhere else. When you need special trade information, seek new distributors or salespeople; they will supply you with the facts. When you have new products to launch or new promotions to announce, they will give you free publicity in their pages.

That's why it is better to divide your budget—to go less frequently in each so that you can cover them all. However, if your budget is such that you will be spreading your ads too thin—like two times here, two times there —then settle on one magazine. Fewer than three insertions is a waste. The frequency figure that produces the best results is six.

WHAT SIZE AD?

Full pages are lovely but not necessary as a steady diet. The best method is to launch with a full-page ad—start out the year with a splash—and then go to island-half sizes and maybe throw in another full page later on.

The island-half is a pet size of mine. It's bigger and costs more than a half and is smaller and costs less than two-thirds. The advantage of this unique unit is that its shape makes it almost impossible to have another ad on the page. You dominate in a solo spot, happily surrounded by editorial matter.

Another striking and economical technique is to use two vertical halves on facing pages (or one-third and two-thirds) with no other ads on the spread. Of course, you have to request this setup. And although you would be taxed an additional charge for such premium positioning in a consumer publication, trade magazines are more cooperative and generally impose no extra tariff. It's a great way to command a double-page spread for the price of a single page.

Now, here's the budget bonus in this split-page method. If you were to run full pages in six issues, you would be billed at a six-time rate. But two facing halves in six issues count as twelve insertions, and you would earn the lower twelve-time rate!

How to take over a full page while paying for just half . . . the island-half ploy

Combination Buy: One-third plus two-thirds pages can dominate a two-page spread . . . and you pay for only one page.

30

Sometimes you may have to go to quarter pages. Okay, if you must, you must, although most publications stack up one quarter-page ad atop another, and you never know where your ad begins and the guy in the upper bunk leaves off. But at least the size is adequate to use readable-sized type and show a decent-sized picture.

But I'd say to skip one-sixth and one-eighth pages in trade magaines. Those small units get buried in the back and always convey a little, unprepossessing impression. Why spend money to let everyone know that you can't afford to spend more?

REPEAT, REPEAT, REPEAT

You have seen the ad at least four times before it hits print. Then you check it again in proof form. By the time it's out, you and everyone at the office are sick of it. After it appears once, the tendency is to say: "Not that ad again! Let's have something new." But that's wrong.

Actually, the ad hasn't even started to reach all the customers, let alone saturate the market. Your personal overexposure is causing you to commit the common sin of public underexposure. A print ad should appear and appear and reappear; in other words it should be seen at least three times.

Do you notice how frequently a single TV commercial is repeated? And do you also notice how your kids can soon recite some TV spots verbatim? That hammering-away repeater technique is motivated by marketing know-how, not frugality. They don't change the commercial after a few showings as soon as you are tired of it. They keep pounding away until you're sick of it. At that point they know the message has sunk in.

Print advertising works the same way. The constant repetition is vital to get your message to saturate the market and become planted firmly in the buyers' minds. As a rule of thumb, when you are just about sick of an ad, it's just about reaching the customer. So let it run, let it run, let it run. And look at the money you save!

TIMING: WHEN TO ADVERTISE

If your big buying season is in spring, you would naturally schedule your ads during the spring months. Hit them when they're ready to buy—that's the rule.

Then there are the big trade shows. I opt for using the issue just prior to the show so the buyer can read your ad before he departs from home, when he's making his little preshow notes and schedules of what and whom to see.

As for those big-show issues that are distributed at the show—those the magazines make such a hullabaloo about —sure, they give out a zillion extra copies at the show, and you get that big zillion bonus circulation; but how many are *distributed* and how many are *read* are two different propositions. Garbage cans don't send in orders, and that's where they often end up.

People at a show just don't have the time or inclination to read trade magazines. And when they get back to their rooms, they're usually exhausted or otherwise occupied and tend to confine their reading to the room-service menus.

Now many magazines put out daily newspapers at the trade shows. Those are well read because they're current, they're fast, and every guy hopes to find his picture in it.

REMEMBER THE REGIONALS

If there are regional magazines in your industry, give them a break. The South and the West seem partial to this sort of homespun gazetteering. And though these regional trade magazines merely duplicate the circulation you are reaching in the national publications, they command a local loyalty you cannot ignore. Besides, their rates are moderate. And if you should open a branch there or have any newsworthy action in the vicinity, they'll be on the spot with photographers and reporters and give you publicity treatment worthy of the opening of a Hollywood delicatessen.

CONSUMER ADVERTISING—THE BIG TIME

Just so you have some idea of how big the big time can get, here are the tariffs some of the popular publications exact for the privilege of displaying your wares among their pages:

Time: One page costs $24,640. (That's only for one week. By the following week your ad is already obsolete.)

Reader's Digest: One page (are you ready?) costs $51,375.

Of course, fractional sizes are less. The smallest *Time* size, a half column (which measures a mere 2¼" by 5"), will set you back $4,620.

Next time you flip casually through a consumer magazine, go slowly. At those prices each ad deserves at least a lingering glance.

The purpose of consumer advertising is to create acceptance and demand for your product or service at the critical spot—the point of purchase (at the store)—in other words to entice the populace into stores to ask for your product or at least to recognize the name when they see it.

To create such a demand requires repetition and a consistent advertising program in magazines, newspapers, and TV—and about $250,000. So we'll drop the dreams and get down to reality.

There are ways to use the big-name publications, even on a budget.

Geographic and Demographic Editions

If your product or service appeals to a selected type of audience or a specifically located audience, you're in luck. Almost all of the big consumer publications offer the opportunity to buy selected segments of their total circulation—at prices far lower, of course, than the national rates.

Geographic editions allow you to place your ad where your buying audience lives. Your ad will appear only in copies of the publication that are distributed in certain cities or states.

For instance, *Reader's Digest* offers ten regional editions: New England, Metropolitan New York, Great Lakes, Southern, North Central, Southwest, Pacific, Metropolitan Los Angeles, Mid-Atlantic, and Metropolitan Chicago. It also offers ten major markets: Metropolitan New York, Metropolitan Los Angeles, Metropolitan Chicago, Boston, Cleveland, Detroit, Philadelphia, Pittsburgh, San Francisco/ Oakland, and Washington, D.C./Baltimore.

The *Wall Street Journal* offers four editions—Eastern, Midwest, Southwest, and Pacific. *Time* offers seven regional and thirteen metropolitan editions. And so on.

Demographic editions allow you to place an ad based on how your audience lives. The breakdowns are according to profession, pursuit, or income. *Time* has three demographic issues: doctors, educators, and students. *Reader's Digest* demos according to income—fifteen thousand a year and over.

Think of the many ways you can use this select-a-market opportunity. Suppose you were selling vacation cottages, the second home no family should be without. Even if you could afford the *Reader's Digest* national rate, you wouldn't want to pay for the wasted circulation of millions of middle Americans who are having a rough time paying for their first homes. With the demographic edition that hits the fifteen-thousand-a-year-and-overs, you would be most likely reaching your ideal potential purchasers. The demographic edition costs $9,640 a page (you can't buy less than a page in demographic or geographic editions). Not exactly peanuts—but a long way from fifty grand.

Or say you are a new company who has just gone public, and you'd like to catch the eyes of some Wall Street wonder lad who might latch on to your stock and zoom it. You would run your ad in the Eastern edition of the *Wall Street Journal* and pay $2,000 for a respectable-sized quarter-page ad, as opposed to $5,000 nationally.

All this information on rates and editions appears in the *Standard Rate & Data, Consumer Magazine* issue (the orange volume).

Amortizing a Consumer Ad

You can get tremendous mileage out of a single consumer ad if you play your collateral material right. A large ad in the right publication can be merchandised to the hilt and used to any number of advantages—for example, as the basis of a campaign to buy admission to a new market.

We had a client who imported cookware and longed to proselytize among that group of rich, ripe consumers—the brides.

Until you get involved with the bridal market, you have no real concept of the kind of wild spending that goes on there. When you realize that every bride is ready and raring to buy a lifetime full of furnishings within a few short months, you get some idea of what kind of sales potential exists for manufacturers of housewares and home furnishings.

And it isn't just what the brides themselves buy. Today, wedding gift-giving has been honed into an efficient system that eliminates any possibility of poor choices (and all elements of sentiment). It's called the Bridal Registry. This procedure has the bride-to-be "registering" her gift preferences in the shop of her choice. Months before the wedding, she calls upon the store's bridal-registry department; there she is greeted like visiting royalty and taken on a personal guided tour of the various departments to select her preferences in every facet of furnishings, from china to cheese boards. The accompanying bridal representative carefully chronicles the choices on a printed registry form, and then wedding guests-to-be are notified that "the bride is registered at ——— store." This enables them to phone the store and say, "What does she want that costs twenty-five dollars and nobody else has bought yet?"

As you can see, it's all heart . . . and big business.

The aim of our client, as of every household-equipment manufacturer, was to get his brand name specified on the bride's registry form. After all, she's the purchasing agent, and her specification means sure sales.

How to get to the bride was easy. There are two bride magazines that are read avidly by every young woman who has set the date, not to mention her mother (this is one pass-along circulation that's valid). The real problem was how to get to the bridal-registry-service representatives and to the store buyers.

Here's how one ad did the job. We used four-color because the outstanding asset of the cookware was its vibrant colors: To use black-and-white would have saved money but lost the campaign. At the bottom of the ad was the fiendishly clever hook:

FREE GIFT FOR YOU

Fill in and mail this coupon now, and we'll send a valuable "whatever-you-wish dish" to your Bridal Registry store IN YOUR NAME. Pick it up whenever you wish.

Name ....

Address ....

My Store ....

The strategy was this:

1. The store bridal consultant would be put in the pleasant position of presenting her bridal customer with a gift, which cost the store nothing (and in so doing, would become aware of the line of cookware).

2. The bride-to-be would be introduced to the advantages of the cookware and possibly induced to specify it in her registry listing.

3. The manufacturer would have an opening wedge to the formerly closed doors of the store cookware buyers.

Before the ad appeared, we made sure to avail ourselves of every facility offered by the magazine's merchandising department. And that is a bargain benefit not to be overlooked. Every good consumer publication has a department devoted to producing material and services to promote the products advertised in their pages. Reprints, preprints, mailings, listings in newsletters, presentations to store buyers—their cooperation is boundless and nominal. Thus we were able to obtain full-color preprints of the ad and mounted counter cards at unbelievably low prices. The material was distributed by the company salesmen and also mailed to bridal-registry departments throughout the country.

The promotion was a huge success. The ad pulled one of the highest reader responses ever recorded by the magazine (it happened to be a great ad), and gift dish packages, including brochures of the full line of cookware, were sent to thousands of young women via their bridal registries. As a result, the manufacturer gained entry into the bridal registry of nearly every major department store in the country.

COOPERATIVE ADVERTISING

It's always nice to have someone else share expenses. It allows you to spread your budget so much farther.

If you sell a product or service to dealers, cooperative advertising is of great benefit to you. If you are the dealer who resells the product or service, cooperative advertising is of great benefit to you. This is one arrangement where everybody wins.

The procedure is just what the name implies. The dealer runs ads, usually in his local media, for which the manufacturer picks up part of the tab. The manufacturer loves it because the ads promote his products in more media than he could otherwise afford to reach. And the dealer loves it because it enables him to afford to run ads that promote his name and bring in business.

If you are the manufacturer, encourage your dealers to take advantage of your cooperative-advertising program. Offer to pay 15 percent, 25 percent, or 50 percent—whatever you feel you can afford—of the cost of the space or time purchased by the dealer to promote your products. Payment is made, either in cash or in merchandise credit, upon submission of bills from the media.

To make it easier for the dealer and to insure that your product is shown and described as you would like, offer prepared artwork and newspaper mats. Mats are the paper plates from which newspapers print. Any engraver will make mats from your finished art.

If you are the dealer, ask your suppliers for all the co-op help possible. It's one of those happy arrangements that are good for both of you.

Chapter 3

PURCHASING TECHNIQUES

"One hundred and fifty dollars for preparation for that little ad? And what's a mechanical and a velox anyway?"

When you don't know what you're buying, you can feel put upon even when the bill is eminently fair. And that sort of misunderstanding between supplier and client can cripple advertising and sales-promotional efforts.

It's hard for a businessman who deals in concrete objects to understand the basis for bills for intangibles such as talent and creativity. Manufacturing a handbag, now that's easy to price: so much for raw materials, so much for labor, so much for overhead, commissions—and there's your price. And look at what you've got—a solid, beautiful product that you can use, touch, and enjoy. But some cut-up pieces of words pasted on a board that you call a mechanical? What's it worth?

Let's start with an explanation of what goes into the creation and production of advertising to give you some idea of what you're paying for—and then later along, how those prices are arrived at. So that you understand all the items you will find listed on your advertising bills, here is an informal glossary of the terms used in ad preparation.

GLOSSARY OF OFT-USED AD TERMS

AA's: Author's alterations. This means changes that originated from you, due either to your original errors or to later corrections and additions.

Benday: A screen process that is applied to black type or black areas to make them gray. Various gradations of grays can be achieved this way, from very light to almost black. It is a method of getting a two-tone effect from one color ink.

Binding: The stitching together of pages into a catalog or booklet. Stapled, wire-bound, or plastic-bound are the most common techniques.

Bleed: When the printed area goes right flush up to the edge, as though it runs off the page. This costs more in printing or in media advertising, because it necessitates the use of more paper.

Blueprint: The proofs supplied in offset printing. It can show only one color, blue, but is usually adequate to judge if everything is properly placed.

Camera-ready: Completed artwork, ready for the printer to set before his camera to convert into printing negatives and plates.

Coated stock: Paper with a shiny finish. It comes coated on one side or both sides.

Cold type: The new less expensive way of typesetting. It's done with a typewriter instead of hot metal, and the results are rarely as good as hot type. You don't get perfect spacing, and the varieties of typefaces are still rather limited. However, it's good enough for many purposes such as price sheets, specification sheets, technical literature, and other quick-and-dirty work that doesn't require classy type.

Comp: A comprehensive of a design for presentation. It usually means a fairly tight rendering of what the finished piece of advertising will look like, and some of the comps I've seen look even better than the finish. Comps are submitted to the client for projected ads, direct mail, literature, displays. If it's a true comp, it costs—because much time is expended in its preparation. So if you can stretch your imagination a little, settle for a "rough" (which is a primitive version of a comp); you'll save a bundle.

Cut: Another name for metal engraving used in letterpress printing. You see less and less of this term as one magazine after another has been changing over to offset printing.

Die-cutting: Mechanical cutting of cardboard or paper into shapes. When you want anything other than square, straight edges, it must be die-cut.

Engraving: Same as a cut.

Font: A whole typeface—from A to Z. Each style of type is called a font.

Galley proofs: Sheets of rough paper that show all the set type you ordered, but not yet set up into proper page form. When doing a catalog or booklet that will undergo many revisions, it's wise to ask the typographer for galley proofs first. It's cheaper to make corrections at this early stage than it is after the type has been set up into page form.

Halftone: Printed reproduction of a photograph. It requires tone patterns and screening and special negatives. Naturally, it's more expensive than straight type. In printing, your price is affected by the number of halftones included.

Laid finish: A fine finish to paper. You see a nice pattern effect of vertical and horizontal lines.

Layout: The design for any piece of advertising.

Line copy: Typography is line copy; black-and-white drawings are line copy. Any composition of solid black without gradations of tone is line copy.

Lithography: Another word for offset printing.

Logo: Short for logotype. The distinctive design symbol or style of type associated with the company name.

Mat: Paper plate used for reproducing art in newspapers. When you are inserting ads in newspapers, you must have an engraver convert your artwork into a metal plate first, and from that, a mat.

Matte finish: Dull finish paper.

Mechanical: Finished board with camera-ready art in place.

Mezzotint: A line print made from a photograph. It makes the picture look like an etching—very arty and effective.

Multilith: An inexpensive process of printing up to 8½" by 11" pieces in small quantities. Not recommended when a quality look is sought, since halftones always come out weaker and missing detail and sharpness.

Offset: Printing that requires no costly metal plates. It has become the prevalent process of printing today and has gradually replaced the older, more expensive letterpress method.

Paste-up: Another word for mechanical.

Pica: Unit of measurement used in typesetting and printing. Six picas equal one inch.

Press proof: Proofs actually made while the job is on press. Usually used to check colors, quality of halftones —a last-minute check before the printing run begins.

Production: This is the work involved in transforming a design into reality. It covers specifying sizes and styles of type, getting the type set and back and pasted up, arranging for photostats, photographs, and veloxes—in short, pulling together all the elements required to produce an ad or piece of advertising material.

Repros: The usual term for the typographer's glossy sheets of set type.

Retouching: Airbrushing photographs to blow out the eyesores and sharpen the strong points. Almost every photo needs a bit of retouching to provide highlights the camera may have overlooked or to straighten ragged edges that the camera did not overlook.

Reverses: The white-on-black areas in printing, as when white type appears against a black background.

Rough: A rough version of a layout. Not as fancy and exact as a comp. The words may be designated as just lines and the photos as sort of shaped smears, but usually quite adequate for visualizing the finished product.

Saddle-stitching: Binding with wire staples, as used in most magazines.

Screens: The coarseness or refinement in the density of a halftone is determined by its screen number; 150 screen is finer than 85 screen. The number describes the dots per linear inch. (If you look at any printed photograph through a magnifying glass, you will see the dots.) Those used for newspapers, 55 to 85 screens, are coarser. For printing fine-quality halftones in magazines and literature, 100 to 150 screens are used.

Serifs and sans serifs: A serif typeface has a little stroke projecting from the top and bottom of each letter. A sans serif has none.

Silhouette halftone: When the tonal background is completely deleted and only the subject is shown against a solid of black, white, or color. This silhouetting can be done right on the photograph or by the printer.

Silk-screen: A form of stencil printing used on cardboard or wood. Used primarily for signs and displays.

Square halftone: When the photograph is printed as is, in a square or rectangular shape.

Stuffer: Small circulars for stuffing in invoice envelopes. Usually supplied by manufacturers gratis to retailers for distribution to the store customers.

Tear sheet: The magazine page containing your ad. Supplied free by the publication.

Vandyke: Same as a blueprint, only in brown ink instead of blue.

Velox: Print of a photograph which has been prescreened before it reaches the printer. It saves you the higher expense involved when the printer does the screening. However, if you don't have a skilled velox-maker in your area, let the printer do it. A poor velox can kill your details and result in a murky halftone.

CREATIVITY—THE INTANGIBLE

They don't sell paintings by the pound. The value of a creative effort is not measured by size or weight.

When you buy a layout, copy, or design, you are paying for three things:

1. Time the artist or writer spent creating the concept.

2. Actual hours expended in physical execution of the idea.

3. Years spent developing the talent that enabled him or her to produce this creative effort.

The first item—creative time—is not computed with a stop watch, of course. That would be insanity, since some ideas come in seconds, and some take days to jell. And you cannot put a meter on the brain. The second item is evaluated on a time basis. But it is the third point that makes up the bulk of the price.

Many years ago my father demurred at the bill for one hundred dollars presented him by the medical specialist who paid a ten-minute visit to our home to diagnose my brother's mononucleosis. He said, "But, Doctor, one hundred dollars for only ten minutes?"

The doctor answered, "Ten minutes here, yes—but what about the thirty years of training and experience that qualified me to make that ten-minute diagnosis?"

It's the years of working with accounts and learning which approach sells, what the customers want to know that will make them buy, what merchandising elements must be considered, how your sales story should be presented to get the greatest possible sales mileage—that's the intangible that makes the difference.

A new client once complained to me about the costs of preparing a series of ads and compared them to lower bills he had received from the ad agency he had recently left. So we compared the former ads to the new ones.

The products were English riding wear. The old ads used line drawings (cheaper to reproduce than photographs) which looked as though they had been done in a high-school art-class exercise. The new ads used high-style photographs of the boots and breeches in action. The old ad for rubber riding boots showed a pair of boots and was headed, "Protection in the Rain," which automatically restricted sales of these boots to the rainy-day category.

Our ad for the same boots showed them on a young rider, sitting on a stable fence against a gray, but not rainy, sky. The ad was headed, "All weather that looks like all leather." Here was an immediate expansion of sales horizons by indicating that these smart-looking boots not only are for slopping about in the rain, but are handsome footwear to be worn with pride in rain, snow, sun, or anytime.

The client looked at both ads side by side, and then we asked the critical question: "Which ad sold more boots?" He just smiled and never brought up the comparison price business again.

I am not saying that you must expect or accept any price. That kind of blank-check ordering is for millionaires or fools or both. You are entitled to, and certainly should ask for, an estimate on any creative effort. But just don't compare apples and oranges.

We have basic prices for layout, copy, production, and mechanical for an 8½" by 11" piece, an 11" by 17" piece, and so on. By now, we pretty much know how long it should take from start to finish and have priced accordingly. Sometimes it takes longer, and we lose a little. Sometimes it goes faster, and we win a little. It all evens out in the long run. Most advertising agencies have set figures for their services that vary according to the caliber of the talent employed, and thus inevitably, the quality of the work produced.

HOW TO TELL GOOD FROM BAD
WHEN BUYING ADVERTISING SERVICES

Printing

A well-printed piece is like a well-turned-out woman: you know she looks great, but you can't figure out just why. It's all a matter of skillfully, subtly executed details. But if you examine the piece closely, you will notice that (1) the photographs are sharply defined and sparkling with contrast; (2) the colors are solid and strong; the red is really red, the black is pure black; (3) the register is right, which means that solid areas butt up to each other perfectly—there's no overlap that causes fuzzy, sloppy-looking edges.

A poorly printed piece has been run through the press fast. That's how come the lower price; press-time charges can be lower. Photos and colors are usually somewhat muddy. They use inexpensive inks that dry fast without giving good solid coverages. They've skimped on the caliber of the printing negatives, so you get dull gray halftones.

And there's often an irregularity in the quality of all the printed material delivered. Since they can't always afford to wait for the full colors to come through on the ink rollers before they start the run, the first batches that come off the press may not have perfect ink coverage and look pale and cheesy.

There can be a large disparity in prices between a good printer and a cheap house. I am not recommending one over the other, because not every piece requires high-quality printing. And not everyone cares. But there is a standard of quality below which no company should go. There's a large difference between a functional, commercial piece of literature and a shoddy one. You are poorly represented by a shoddy one. Ask for estimates before you buy, and ask for samples of the printer's work. I have explained all the differences to you so that before you decide on the cheaper source, you will be aware of how much the savings will cost you.

Photography

A good photographer will fuss with lighting and with lenses. He'll take time to position the subject intelligently. He will recognize which imperfection will be exposed by the camera's merciless eye. He has an eye for composition and will produce a nicely balanced shot.

A poor photographer, due to ignorance, laziness, or inability to afford the time, will not bother to do anything more than plunk your product in front of the camera, turn on the existing bank of lights, and shoot. The results: (1) The unpretty guts of the product show; (2) the irregular stitching that he could have turned to hide is glaringly obvious; (3) the deliveryman's greasy thumbprints have not been wiped off.

The difference in price between a good commercial photographer and a poor one is negligible—maybe no

Poor Photography: Note the overlighted background showing pipes, electrical box, and other unlovely details. Also see the unflattering angle that shows both product and model at worst possible advantage.

Good Photography: How much happier the product and model look. Note how the picture captures the gleam of the stainless steel . . . how the background recedes rather than intrudes.

more than ten dollars for a product shot. Any saving is lost when you pay the bill for retouching required to make the photo usable.

Sometimes it's not even price. Photography is a talent; one guy has it, and the other just doesn't. So before you select a commercial photographer, take a minute to look over his samples. Check for the points I mentioned. See if the photos are sharp, artistic, and flattering. And when you give him his first assignment, go to his studio to supervise and guide. Point out what facets of the subject are to be stressed and which played down. He can't possibly know, for example, that the unfinished raw-looking edge of a pot is really a chip-resistant rim that is your big selling feature. And perhaps you want the box to be included, too.

The studio is the preferred place to shoot, since the best lighting equipment is there. However, if you have heavy machinery that is unfeasible to transport, or if you have a large number of awkward objects to photograph, it might be more convenient to have the photographer come to your place to shoot. The photos will rarely turn out as well, since the lighting is only functional and the backgrounds are usually ghastly. But if you must, you must.

Once you have established relations with a photographer and he gets to know what you want, you can just send stuff over with a very rough sketch, and more than likely, you will get satisfactory results.

There are all kinds of specialists in photography: fashion, location, food, architecture, aerial, and so on. If you're fortunate, you will find one fellow who is competent in all the areas you need. I say "competent" because there's almost no ceiling to photography charges. There are men that ask, and get, a thousand dollars a day for shooting. I watched one of the world's most famous photographers work over the shooting of a single piece of IBM equipment for hours, and he told me that he had been at it since the previous day. Just an ordinary little gray desk-top machine, and each photo that he had discarded looked like a minor masterpiece to me. But he wasn't satisfied yet. But then, IBM could afford to pay for the photographer's indulging himself in the luxury of achieving perfection.

For small business use, where we don't anticipate using a photo in a two-page spread in *Time*, genius is not a requirement. Just reasonable talent and competence.

Photo-Retouching

It's usually necessary to retouch a photo somewhat— just a bit of airbrushing here and there to deaden or delineate detail. The better the photograph, the less re-touching needed, of course. But when you do, make sure you find a retoucher who has a *light* touch. That's the quality that makes the difference. A skilled artist air-brushes smoothly graduated tones and subtle highlights, so that the retouching is almost impossible to detect; you just end up with a clear, sharp, beautiful photograph. A lousy retoucher will go heavy on the white paint, will leave strong blocks of darks, will make highlights look like white streaks, and you end up with a clunky picture that more resembles a rendering than a photograph.

Remember that there are specialists in retouching as well as in photography. Some are great with machinery but can turn humans into death masks. Just be sure you have the right man for the job.

TO BARGAIN OR NOT TO BARGAIN

Many commercial entrepreneur types think it's shrewd to play the heavy businessman when dealing with artists or agencies. They bargain; they haggle. If the artist quotes $350, they "drive the price down" to $300 and feel a sense of businesslike achievement.

But it doesn't work. Bargaining is a bust with a creative

source. You are not dealing with a constant object, but with a finished product that is very much affected by the attitude of the artist who created it. Basically, every artist aims to please himself. He'll work and rework to get a result that comes up to his personal set of standards. But antagonize him at the outset, and you will get first-draft "off the top of the head" thinking. He won't bother with the all-important refinement processes—he won't begrudge you the time.

That doesn't mean that you should not ask for an estimate. Nor to admit that it's more than you are prepared to spend. For example, you might have a limited budget for a specific project. There's no harm in announcing, "Look, I have just three hundred dollars for art on this job. Can you do it for that price?" That's perfectly reasonable, and the artist has the option to turn it down if he finds the price impossible. And chances are, if you have developed a rapport and need a special price, he'll happily accommodate, providing you don't pull that poor-mouth too often.

But once you have a working relationship with an artist, agency, photographer, printer, and you know his prices are fair, don't haggle. It only creates an ill-will that will blow you absolutely no good.

AVOIDING SHAMEFUL WASTE

We have a morgue of dead roughs: my heartbreak file of clever copy and gorgeous graphics that died unborn because of that very expensive type of client exercise—mind-changing.

It's a very costly activity and one you should try to avoid. There's nothing more disheartening and wasteful than spending hours in the creation of a promotion, an ad, a mailer, a whatever, only to have the client call sheepishly to advise that due to circumstances entirely within his control, he no longer needs the piece or he wants it in an entirely different form. He gets charged for the unused work, and it's a total loss to all. Here are some examples of wastes that could have been avoided—and how to do it.

"What we need is a big brochure that shows the whole line so the salesmen can carry it around instead of our big catalog."

Fine. The agency prepares the layout and copy and sends out the rough for the client to look over. Then comes the call: "Er-er . . . we showed the rough to our salesmen and they say it's nice, but they have to carry the big catalog anyway. So I guess we really don't need the brochure."

Why the devil didn't he check with the salesmen before? It's not nice to call the client an idiot, so you mutter something clever about that being the way the cookie crumbles, you wish to hell he would, and you hang up wondering why you didn't go into schoolteaching like your mother urged.

If you think an ad piece is needed, check first with those you think need it *before* you give out the assignment.

"Big news. We've just set up a free-call direct line to our factory to speed up customer service inquiries. Make up a big mailing right away."

The piece gets finished, ready for camera, and then comes the phone call: "Er-er. [Clients usually stammer when they're wrong, I'll say that for them.] We just realized we don't want to push the free phone bit or we'll have every shnorrer chiseler using the phone to phone orders instead of mailing them. Just change the emphasis on the piece, tell 'em to send their orders right to the plant, and mention the free phone casually."

Those little words "change the emphasis" translated into ad language mean "do the whole damned piece over."

If it's something new, think it through *before* you give out the assignment.

Communicate—that's the most important waste preventative of all. If you have something special in mind, take the time to convey it, because even though most advertising folk are talented, perceptive, and sensitive (present company included, of course), mind-reading is not one of the standard trade attributes.

Often you will have a mental image of what you would like to see in a printed piece, a design, a photo, and will tend to judge the value of the results by how close it comes to your preconception. In those situations just take a piece of paper and draw a rough of what you have in mind. I can hear the howls of pain and protest: "Me? Draw? I'm all thumbs. All I can draw is conclusions." No one is expecting a Rembrandt, just a rough-rough that is enough to convey a feeling. This sort of little sketch, no matter how primitive, can be an invaluable guide that may save you and the creative source a pile of porridge.

Communicate your ideas graphically. No matter how primitive, it can do the job.

THE "NEW CORPORATE IMAGE" CRAZE

There comes a moment in the development of every small business when someone says, "What we need is a constant corporate image—a continuity in all our promotional output."

That someone is usually the new sales manager or marketing manager. He's been brought in to beef up sales, to pull together all the amorphous efforts and activities that had been previously handled by a dozen different unqualified people to whom the jobs had fallen by default.

The new man is usually hit all at once with the results of ten years of corporate chaos. He finds he has the bewildering, overwhelming task of converting near-anarchy into a disciplined organization. At about this point one of the corporate-image vendors approaches him with the proposal for a complete evaluation of the corporate image and the evolution of a total graphics approach that will make it all hang together.

The poor guy falls upon the suggestion like he has found his Rosetta stone. It sounds so logical, so comforting—and so impressively big business. So he stumps for it to management and proclaims that the process will be the panacea for all their ills and that, in one step, it will erase the corrosion of years of corporate confusion.

If he wins, the company springs for anywhere from five thousand to ten thousand dollars, and the corporate-image vendors do their stuff.

They usually claim that they must go out into the field and do research studies to get a feel of the market before the proper concept can be achieved. Time passes, sketches are submitted, and ultimately they produce a new "individualized, powerful logo," maybe a stylized rendition of the first letter of the company name or some graphic gimmick to convey the firm's field of endeavor. (The original logo which the company has been using for years may or may not be old-fashioned. That's not always bad. Often it's distinctive, and that's all you want. And more important, everyone recognizes it, is familiar with it. And that's what you want.)

The new logo is hailed as the new cohesive factor in the company and necessitates redesigned letterheads, labels, and packaging. Then comes the recommendation that all company literature and packaging feature a strong familial relationship. Result: good taste and guaranteed monotony.

I'm all for good packaging, but where is it written that they must all look alike or even similar? Nobody buys a product because it looks like another. Every sale is made based on the appeal of that individual item. The only one who truly appreciates a family similarity in packaging is the boss, because it gives him a good feeling to see such a nice, neatly coordinated stockroom.

If you will note the packaging of leading consumer products, every one is handled as an individual product. Resemblance is scrupulously avoided. The name of the game is to stand out, not blend into a shelf of look-alikes.

As for the brand-new logo, do you really think that Westinghouse sales skyrocketed because they paid Paul Rand a fortune to produce the distinctive "W"?

The expenditure of thousands of dollars on a "new corporate image and logo" is a type of indulgence favored by new executives of giant corporations who have money to toss around and a need to justify their new positions. I have never seen any documentation or proof to indicate that a new logo produces profit for anyone but the graphic designers, printers, and packaging companies. For the small business such a project is a useless, nonproductive extravagance.

CHAPTER 4

COPYWRITING

Advertising is somewhat like architecture in one vital respect: The value of the work is judged, not for itself, but for its effectiveness in achieving a specific purpose.

Lincoln Center's Philharmonic Hall in New York City is a classic example of award-winning beauty that didn't work. A stunning edifice, comfortable facilities, fine visibility. Only one thing wrong—you couldn't hear the music well.

How many times have you admired an ad for its cleverness, its outstanding graphics, and then ten minutes later, realized you didn't know what the ad was selling? This sort of fiasco is usually the product of a series of Madison Avenue mutual-massaging-of-the-ego sessions. Its prime motive, for the creators, is to win accolades from their peers. The client is expected to bask in their reflected glory and pride of artistic achievement when his company's ad wins an award.

We of the small budgets consider this the lowest form of sophistry. In our pragmatic world the success of any ad is measured by one yardstick only: sales. Art is never for art's sake; art is solely for the sake of the man or woman who's paying the bills.

There is a classic advertising-agency ad that has been repeated time and time again over the past twenty-five years. It show two identical photos of a man sitting in an armchair reading a newspaper. The first picture is captioned: "Gosh, this is a great ad!" The second picture is captioned: "Gosh, this is a great product!" The explanation beneath both, of course, indicates that this ad agency supports the second position. So do I. So must you.

> Basic copywriting rule 1: You can be creative
> and clever in smaller-budget advertising. But
> none of these aims must be allowed to over-
> shadow the prime purpose of the ad—*to sell.*

SMALL AND HONEST

There's no doubt that people are impressed and somewhat cowed by four-color double-page spreads. Bigness conveys wealth, wealth means success, and success means they're good—or how else did they get so big?

That's the big hurdle in smaller-budget advertising—to convey solidity and reliability in a big way but in small space.

As every con man knows, if you want to hook a mark, do it big. Most people have an implicit trust in vastness. That's why the con-type ads are usually big and flashy. You've undoubtedly seen the ads that sell palm-tree-studded sites in some Florida swamp, or the ads that offer inflatable overalls to deflate your overweight. You'll notice they all go in for full-page ads in *Time*, *Life*, and other high-priced media. They have to.

When you have something solid and reliable to sell, you can do it very successfully in more modest space. However, since you do not have the credibility factor of bigness to impress the reader, you must do it with absolute honesty. No overstated claims, no lavish promises, no implausible statements. Once a shred of disbelief enters the reader's mind, the entire ad crumbles. The big guys can afford a little exaggeration here and there, but we can't. Like Caesar's wife, we have to be above suspicion.

> Basic copywriting rule 2: In small business honesty is not the best policy—it is the only policy. Dramatize, elaborate, but never overrate or overstate.

HOW TO WRITE COPY THAT SELLS

It isn't difficult to write copy that sells, and it really doesn't require great genius. The most important part of writing good copy is evolving the right approach, the basic appeal that touches closest to the heart of the buyer. It is a distillation process, a careful analysis of the product or service you are selling and of the needs of the people who will be buying it.

STEP 1: *Analyze your product or service.* Evaluate its features, and list every conceivable service it performs for the user. For example, you have a laundry: You turn out finely finished work; you pick up and deliver; you replace broken and lost buttons. You have a local gift shop: You carry a highly selective group of items from leading manufacturers as well as an eclectic array of contemporary handicrafts. You manufacture lamps: You feature a special patented design light that has spring-controlled extending arms. You manage a local bank: You offer many loan services plus personalized advice on family finance and money management. You distribute plumbing supplies: You carry a huge stock of the best lines available; you guarantee shipment the same day an order is received.

STEP 2: *Translate these product features into terms of*

end-user benefits. Now that you know what your product does, figure out what tangible benefits these features mean to potential buyers. Nobody much cares that your product or service is great unless they know what great things it can do for them. You must sell the benefit, not the product.

Following up on the previous examples, let's start with the laundry. What can your finely finished work, pickup and delivery, and button-sewing service mean to the house-wife? Answer: (1) tremendous convenience, (2) more leisure time, (3) happier husband (fewer complaints) and smoother homelife.

The gift shop: What can your eclectic array of gifts mean to the shopper? Answer: (1) elimination of the wear and tear of traveling downtown, (2) The convenience of one-stop shopping for all gifts.

The lamp-manufacturer: What benefits can a lamp that stretches bring to a user? Answer: (1) ideal for children who like to squirm about when reading, (2) gives them better light, better studying conditions.

The local bank: What does the personal touch of dealing with a local bank mean? Answer: (1) It's easier to get a loan because the bank knows you and your standing in the community; (2) you avoid the unpleasant hat-in-hand posi-tion required when you walk in cold to a strange bank.

The plumbing distributor: What can your high-quality merchandise and fast delivery mean to the local plumber? Answer: (1) confidence that he won't get complaints about equipment after he has installed it, (2) better, faster service to his customers as a result of immediate delivery.

> Basic copywriting rule 3: Evaluate your prod-ucts, and translate the benefits into values the customer can readily identify with. Don't just think of what the product does, but what it does for the user.

STEP 3: *You know what to say; how should you say it? Now that you have assembled your arsenal of facts and the slant to be used, it is time to arrange it in ad form.*

The headline: Take your prime user benefit, and convert it into as succinct a statement as you can. Tell it, and tell it fast. For instance, here are some possibilities: The laundry: "We free you for the better things in life." The gift shop: "The Right Gift . . . in the Right Place . . . Right here on Main Street." The lamp-manufacturer: "The Activist—the lamp that follows the student movement." The bank: "Of course we'll help out with money. That's what neighbors are for!" The plumbing distributor: "Order Today—Install Tomorrow."

These are just some suggestions to give you an idea of procedure. If you think about them and doodle about a bit, you will come up with dozens of possible headlines for these ad situations. They don't all have to be declarative statements; questions are great stoppers. But try it; it's good brain exercise, and it gets your mind moving into the right channels for copywriting.

As a real-life postscript to the hypothetical situations I've used above, you might be interested in some actual headline approaches that proved highly successful. The Redactron Corporation introduced an editing typewriter, which consists of an automatic typewriter that works together with a magnetic tape or card unit. The Redactron does a miraculous job of making revisions and retyping, completely automatically. It can accelerate the typing output of any size secretarial staff. All right, that's what it does. Now what can that mean to the office manager in a context that he will immediately recognize?

The headline that did it was "How to get 65 hrs. of typing from every 35-hr.-a-week typist."

Since office managers have trouble these days getting thirty hours of work from a thirty-five-hour-a-week typist, the headline was a real grabber. Also, the use of the word "every" indicated that no special training was required to operate the machine; every typist could handle it.

The Environmental Farms of Tucson had developed a new kind of tomato that was being grown in the most fantastically controlled conditions science and nature could produce. Because of their carefully nurtured situation, they could be picked ripe (instead of the usual green) and would be flown to market within a day.

Now, how to convey, in one headline, that here was a new, luscious, extraordinarily tasty tomato?

The headline arrived at was, "Introducing . . . the brand-new vegetable/fruit tomato," and showed a wholesome young girl biting into it as you would an apple. What was instantly conveyed was: Here's a unique tomato that's sweet and delicious as a piece of fruit. This headline became their slogan and went into all their ads and on packaging as well.

The body of the ad: Okay, you have stopped the reader with your headline. What do you do next? You sell him or her. You enumerate all the advantages your headline has promised in short, terse sentences, with no wasted words. Keep it spare, keep it lean, and keep it direct.

After you have written a first draft, go over it again and again to weed out all the unnecessary words. It's easy to write a long ad; what's hard is to produce a short one. Don't be afraid to use phrases and incomplete sentences. Your fifth-grade teacher isn't around to fault you on grammar and to insist on perfectly formed syntax. Sometimes the use of a phrase gives a nice clipped pace that makes for easier reading. For example, "It's a handsome coat. And lightweight, too." Somehow that looks better and reads faster than: "It's a handsome coat, and it is lightweight, too."

The hook: By now, they're primed, they're convinced; they want whatever it is you're selling. What do they do now to get it?

Never, never write an ad, a sales letter, a presentation, any piece of advertising, without in some way instructing the reader of the step he or she must take in order to see or buy or get further facts about the product. Any advertising that omits this basic information is a waste of the reader's time and a waste of the advertiser's money.

Decide what action you want them to take, and ask them to do it. If you want inquiries so that you can pass the sales leads on to your salesmen, ask them to write in for literature. If you want them to go out and buy the product, tell them where. If you want them to send in an order, ask them to do it at once.

Whatever you want the readers to do, *tell them plainly at the bottom of the ad.* If you can offer some special incentive to motivate them to act immediately, before they put the ad aside and possibly forget it, so much the better.

"Bring in this ad and get $1.00 off."

"Order now and get free gift."

"Buy now while special-price sale is on."

> Basic copywriting rule 4: Don't be bashful; ask for the order.

SUPPLEMENTARY COPYWRITING TIPS

Use Humor

The light touch can be very effective—unless you're selling burial plots. It suspends disbelief and makes you more likable and somewhat more credible. Most people, as you know, mistrust advertising statements. A bit of humor that shows you are real folks, not some pompous corporate body, lowers the anti-advertising guard a bit and allows acceptance to sneak in.

There are lots of ways to use humor. If you have an odd name, a laughable name, you can turn it into an asset by owning up to it and treating it lightly. "With a name like Smuckers, it's got to be good."

Or you can show comic-tragic situations people can get themselves into when they do not use your product, such as that great series of ads by Talon that portrayed the embarrassing positions one can be caught in when a critical zipper breaks.

Puns can be attention-getting. We once used what could be a dreadful pun, because it was going to a pun-apprecia-tive audience. We were promoting an academic-year calen-dar to college students. The aim of the piece was to point out the hazards of being unaware of days and dates. The heading was, "Summa Cum Later," which may make you wince but made them buy a helluva lot of calendars.

If you have an uninteresting product, humor can take the curse off it. If the medium you are using, or the market you are hitting, is burdened with dull, super-serious ma-terial (ever look through some of the engineering maga-zines?), an injection of lightness can make your ad stand out.

Don't Fuss over Quality

Just as every mother tells you that her child is the great-est, so every seller announces that his product is the best. Both of these statements, when made publicly, are con-sidered equally objective and equally believable.

How many times have I asked a client, "In what ways is your product better?" and gotten the answer: "In every way. It's the finest-quality product in the industry."

Terrific.

In many cases it may be perfectly true, but general state-ments of excellence are totally unconvincing. That doesn't mean that you should ignore the quality factor. Not at all —it's very important. But the only way to convey superiority and get some credibility is with specific claims. Select particular features, individual aspects that you can point up, and then translate them into the direct benefits the buyer will derive from these higher-quality factors.

For example, if you are selling English riding breeches that are made by England's finest tailors, you could just state that fact: "Tailored by England's finest riding-wear craftsmen." Nice. Dignified. But so what? This type of statement usually pleases the manufacturer because it has the classy ring he likes. But rarely does it have any effect on prospective purchasers. Not unless you distill the fact into what it can mean to the user: "Incredibly cut by England's finest tailors to give you marvelous figure and freedom." Now you have told the purchaser why these breeches are superior and how the superiority affects her.

Sometimes lack of quality is an asset—*if* you make a deliberate point of it and it is a part of your selling story. For example, a client produced cassette transports which computer manufacturers integrate into their units. These transports were of very simple, thus less expensive, construction and performed limited functions. They were designed for the users who needed only those limited functions but who up to now had been forced to buy costly complicated units that offered services they could not use. The lack of quality, reflected in the lower price, was its greatest selling asset.

"Why pay for overcapability?" was the theme of the campaign.

Avoiding the big stress on top quality is sometimes difficult in the arena of small business. Perhaps the reason is the very reason that it is so stimulating working with small business. You usually deal with the founders of the company, the people who were actively involved in its creation and development. Their feelings toward the firm are strongly emotional. They have worked on every facet of its growth and believe implicitly that their product is the very finest of its kind.

Being more objective and having the advantage of dealing with many companies, I know that there is rarely any one finest of its kind. Usually there are a few of comparable excellence, each having different points of superiority. So if you are the company principal, please heed these words; they can save you a lot of money in wasted advertising space: Nobody really cares how well you make your product. All they want to know is how well your product will work for them.

Name the Product

No matter how great your ad, it's a dud if buyers don't remember the product or company name.

One of the best insurances against loss of identity is to put the name right in the headline or slogan. Remember Speidel watchband: "Your watch looks swell when you wear Speidel." And going way, way back: "Sal Hepatica for the smile of health."

In any case, be sure that your product or company name appears clearly and loudly.

Appeal to Emotional Needs

When you are evaluating product benefits, don't overlook the aspects that satisfy emotional needs. These are very powerful sales motivators.

Self-image, snob appeal, peer approval, and the like can be a big driving force to the marketplace. People buy Cadillacs and Mercedes not only because they like driving them—they like owning them. If your product or service is an instrument of prestige, play it up.

If you were promoting a school that trained people for specific fields and professions, you would of course mention the greater income rewards that could lie ahead. But more important, stress the prestige factors appurtenant to their new positions: the alteration in community image when one moves from blue collar to white, the sort of people and jazzy folk you might hobnob with.

One of the big motivational research organizations once came out with the tidbit that a convertible automobile represented a mistress to the male buyer. Now there's an emotional need. You may not find one quite as primordial for your product, but it never hurts to try.

If you have an art gallery, you might point out the intellectual quality original art imparts to your home. If you sell books, you might indicate the high intelligence quotient you will be awarded by visitors who see your well-stocked bookshelves and the greater social acceptance you will have when you can converse about the information you have acquired from the books.

"Be the first on your block" and other appeals to status can have a mighty big pull.

Remember Greed

The profit motive—that's the greatest buying consideration when you are selling to dealers. If someone is buying your product in order to resell it at a profit, then the bigger the profit, the bigger his buying incentive.

If your profit margin is larger than usual, if you offer an extra discount, if you have proof that your merchandise can be moved off the shelves faster, if you are planning to back up your product with an extensive TV campaign that will surely build a huge demand, *tell them.*

But please, if you do not offer any of these higher-profit advantages, don't claim you do because you think it sounds like the right thing to say. If you have no real facts to back up your claim, you'll only destroy your total credibility and the positive effect of your ad.

Avoid Invisible Phrases

There is a host of advertising cliches that I call the invisible phrases because they are so overused that nobody really sees them. The eye just glides over the words without bothering to notify the brain.

Pick up any trade magazine, and count how many times you see these hackneyed no-words:

Fast turnover

Impulse buy-item [that's a special cutie]

Outstanding quality

Fast service

Pioneers in the industry [ugh!]

Leaders in the field [ditto]

Ad nauseam. Avoid them. They are a total waste of space. If you cannot communicate these ideas in a more specific, effective way, don't.

Don't Let Dignity Dull Dynamics

One of the frequent problems I've run into with the small entrepreneur is his super-sensitivity to his dignity—whatever that means. I guess it's like the old story of the millionaire who dresses like a bum. He can afford to. When a rich man wears sneakers with his tuxedo, they call him eccentric. But let some poor schnook dress that way, and he's immediately labeled a slob.

That's the image that troubles the little guy in business. He's afraid to do anything daring or innovative for fear of being accused of cheapness. It reminds me of a party I attended where the bar featured an assortment of anonymous-brand booze. After a few belts one of the guests advised the host, in ringing tones: "Joel, you're not rich enough to serve such cheap Scotch."

There is, after all, some validity to the smaller-business man's concern with his image. As we discussed earlier, he cannot risk dishonesty, and he cannot risk exaggeration. But dignity? There's nothing more stuffy, stultifying, and deadly dull than dignity.

If you allow the misguided belief that dramatic dynamics cannot coexist with dignity in advertising, then you'll be turning out the quickest-to-hit-the-wastebasket material ever produced.

The main object of any piece of promotion is to sell—and subliminally, to convey a corporate image of solidity and reliability. But in order to get anyone to read your message, you must first capture his or her attention, and you can't do that with dignity. I don't mean that you should use garish designs and naked girls. That's lack of taste, not lack of dignity.

Remember that creativity and innovativeness convey the image of an aggressive, progressive live organization, and that's the sort of stuff that moves merchandise.

CHAPTER 5

DIRECT MAIL

Whether it comes from a laundry or a foundry, from a cemetery or a caterer, there's one thing all direct-mail pieces have in common: They aim to induce the recipient to *act now*.

There should be an immediacy about direct mail, an urgency that impels the reader to run out and buy right now. That is its purpose. Print advertising (newspapers and magazines), TV, and radio are used to inform the public that you have a great thing that they cannot seriously contemplate living without and to tell them how to get to the point of purchase.

Direct mail tells the same tale, but it gives them the mechanism for immediate ordering—right in their hot little hands. And if your piece is effective, they will be primed and panting to purchase at once, and the order cards will flow.

That's what your direct mail is supposed to achieve. If the customer reads it.

Too many companies lull themselves into believing that the whole world out there is just dying for their product or service. One of our clients assures us, constantly and solemnly, that all the people on his mailing list will read any printed material that bears his company name, due to the tremendous respect the entire industry has for his firm. Companies have gone bankrupt on such delusions.

The fact is, nobody reads any third-class mail unless you cleverly provoke his interest, hit him in the bankbook, or both. If you want your direct mail to work well for you, it must be attention-getting. Mailing has become incredibly expensive these days, what with postage increases, mailing-house costs, and the like. No small company can afford to waste what is now big money on unread, ineffective mailings.

When you use direct mail, it must be well planned and professionally executed. Don't be tempted to ask your neighbor's son, who everyone claims is another Picasso and has won the local Halloween window-painting contest three years running.

Even if you are a local service or store or restaurant, there's no reason to have your mailings look homemade. Remember that when it arrives at its destination, whether a domestic or a business mailbox, it will be competing with some pretty jazzy-looking material. True, if everyone else's piece is slick, your primitive-looking mailing will stand out. That's great. But there's a big difference between primitive and crude. And, too, you want to be sure that simple and primitive is the image you want to impart. That might be fine for a shop selling quaint crafts or rugged sportswear but not very beneficial for an equipment company that wants to convey precision workmanship.

There's a skill, and thus expense, involved in commercial-art preparation; this is one expense you cannot afford to bypass. And beware of circulars written and designed by local printers. They all have a way of coming out to look like handbills announcing the day's special on ground chuck steak.

Ever get one of those simple little four-color mailings from Time-Life, printed on paper that costs a little less than the Krupp diamond and that opens up to modest mural size? Next time you get one, handle it with respect; it probably costs more than your whole mortgage.

How can you even begin to compete? It's easy. Since you are number 2,000, you try much harder. There are many ways to command attention that are inexpensive, ingenious, resourceful. As a matter of fact, sometimes those elaborate budget-busting jobs, with foldouts and pop-ups, are hoist by their own petards. The recipient often gets so hung-up on the sheer gorgeousness and gimmicks of the piece that he forgets just what it is they are trying to sell him.

Simple can be good. Here are some ways to achieve effectiveness by using cleverness instead of cash.

THE FAMILIAR OBJECT IN THE UNFAMILIAR PLACE

Take an object that it familiar to everyone, and use it in a totally unfamiliar place, in a startlingly unexpected way.

A Paper Bag

Here's one of the commonest things around. A plain paper bag. You see it at home, in the office (usually transporting coffee and a Danish), but how about in with your morning mail?

You can use an ordinary paper bag as an envelope; it's a real stopper, and it works wonderfully (I know, I've used it quite successfully). You print on the outside of the bag, insert your advertising material, staple it, stamp it, and mail it. It's that simple. And extremely startling.

Of course, you don't use the bag without tying it in cleverly in some way with your sales story. Think of the many transitional approaches you can use with "It's in the Bag."

Harkening back to the hypothetical advertisers in the previous chapter:

The laundry: "Our integrity is in the bag. You can be sure it's perfect, clean, and as you like it when it comes in a BonTon Bag."

The plumbing-supply distributor: "Sales are in the bag when your installations contain E-Z plumbing products."

These are just some ideas of the way you can use the bag to pique interest and get your sales story across entertainingly. But whatever you do, don't overdo the metaphor. Just use it for openers, drop it, and let it go at that. There's nothing more sickeningly amateurish than a writer who falls in love with his own metaphor and gets so carried away that you and he both forget whatever it was he was trying to sell. The most overused category of metaphor is the sports one. You know: "We'll carry the ball," "You'll score a touchdown," "You're batting a thousand," ad nauseam until you don't know if they're trying to sell you electrical fixtures or athlete's foot powder.

A Bank Statement

If you were a bank and sent out a bank statement, nobody would bat an eyelash. But if you were a frozen-food distributor and sent out what looked like a bank statement, that would be startling. And it's so easy and inexpensive to do. You merely use the same buff-color and weight paper as the usual bank statement and set it up in columns in bank style, so that it looks exactly like a bank statement. In fact, get an actual statement, and copy the style and format exactly. Except use your company name on top, of course.

Then put your selling pitch in some form that relates to a bank statement. For instance: "Want big orders to build up you $$$ deposits? Push the New Kleer-Vu Photo Albums guaranteed to produce fantastically high rate of interest among your customers. . . ."

But absolute authenticity is the vital word here. It must look exactly like a bank statement. A looks-something-like won't do and loses the whole effect. When the recipient sees that piece on his desk or in his mailbox, he has to get the instant impression that this is an important piece of information from a bank. That means your envelope must be a plain bank-style manila window envelope, with no advertising message on front.

You can bet that envelope will be opened fast, and that means you have accomplished the first aim of direct mail —to get the receiver to *open it.*

While we're in the financial area, how about a ledger sheet? Or a simulated checkbook? Or a bank-deposit slip? They are all easy to obtain and simple to reproduce.

Just get your mind going to all the ordinary objects, which you see and handle day by day, that could be adapted for direct mail.

A Piece of Cloth

Take a piece of cloth, for example, and print your message right on it. Of course, not every printer can print on cloth. We surmounted that problem by contacting a label manufacturer. It was no problem for him to print a 6" by 9" piece of fabric, and we used an opening line something like "Maybe we can't send you from rags to riches, but . . . ."

It was so effective, as a matter of fact, that we used this device a number of ways. Once we used a special soft cloth and had the label-manufacturer pink the edges. At the bottom of the cloth we had a little "P.S." to advise that this cloth could be used as a handy wiper for eyeglasses and should be kept. Which it was, which means our effective direct-mail piece had also gained the added sales-promotional value of becoming an advertising specialty and gave prolonged life to our sales message.

A Photo-Finishing Bag

Developed photos always come in a small bag, right? Actually, if you look at it carefully, it is not a special bag —just an ordinary 5" by 8" envelope with an end opening. If it were blank, you would recognize it as an envelope. But print the whole front with the prescribed photo-finishing pattern of boxes and notations, and—*poof!*—it's a photo-finishing bag.

When you see these photo bags in the photo store or in that shoe box you shove them into when you get home, you would barely notice them. After all, that's where you expect to find them. But in among your mail at the office? Wow! This you gotta see.

Why not send out your direct-mail piece in a simulated envelope? There's nothing to it? Just take one of those bags out of the shoe box, send it to the envelope company, and ask them to reproduce it on the front of a 5" by 8" envelope (substituting your company name for any identifiable photo-finisher). Use the other blank side for addressing, and it will be a guaranteed eye-grabber in any pile of mundane mail.

Of course, the insides of the envelope must follow up on the promise of the outside; otherwise you are obviously trying to fool the recipient with a fake device. And no one likes to be fooled, nor feels very kindly disposed toward the fooler.

(Ever find one of those simulated traffic tickets under

your windshield-wiper that turned out to be an advertisement? After the initial shock, when your heart has resumed its pumping so that enough blood gets to your fingers to enable them to pry the piece from under the wiper, how do you feel when you read: "Here's your ticket to carefree motoring. Drive in now to Joe's Muffler Shop for a free muffler inspection"?

I know I usually feel like driving right in—at sixty miles an hour.)

THE BOLD FOLD

Take an 8½″ by 11″ sheet of paper—the commonest, least expensive size—and fold it twice horizontally, in the commonest style, and what have you got? A one-page letter. Predictable, unimaginative, dull.

Now take that same sheet of paper, and fold it first in half horizontally and then once vertically. What do you have? A many-paged folder. Or an invitation. Or an announcement. Or a greeting card.

Or using that same 8½″ by 11″ sheet, lay it horizontally on your desk, fold it accordian-style, and—*presto!*—a six- or eight-page folder.

Look at all the creative ramifications that can develop from a basic 8½″ by 11″ sheet, and think of all the different design and copy concepts that can emerge.

If you used the 8½″ by 11″ sheet flat, handbill style, you'd end up with just one page (and a back). Each page is viewed as a single entity and must be treated that way. The limitations are obvious: You are restricted to as much or as little as the eye can grasp in one look, and you must rely heavily on graphics to direct the eye from points of major importance to those of lesser value.

But fold the sheet, and you have panels, pages; and you can lead the reader in a selective step-by-step sales-building procedure. Where before, you could only effectively feature one offering on a page and attempt to convey only one concept at a look, now you can show up to eight! Not only have you made the same piece of paper work harder and do more, but you have made it look more impressive. You have endowed it with substance. It's no longer a sheet—it's a brochure.

The Invitation-Style Fold

Here you can use an invitation slant: "We invite you to see the new line of ABC products—right here!"

Or as an announcement: "Announcing an entirely new concept in gift-giving." Of course, this style must be sent out in a matching-style envelope (but more on envelopes farther on).

The Accordion-Style Fold

Fold the sheet three times, hold it vertically, and suddenly you have an eight-page folder—a miniature pocket-sized catalog. Each panel can feature a different product or service, with the front page functioning as a cover. Or fold it twice if you need larger panels.

The Accordion-Style Indexed-Top Fold

Take your accordion-style folder, open it, and make an angle cutoff along the long side of the sheet.

I can just hear the printing cognoscenti out there in readerland saying: "Aha—a die-cut. Now we blow the whole budget!"

Not so. This is a die-cut effect achieved without encountering the die-cutting cost. It never has to leave the printer and be shipped off to the time-consuming, cash-consuming die-cutter—the fellow who uses huge machinery and special dies to cut holes, angles, and shapes in paper and cardboard.

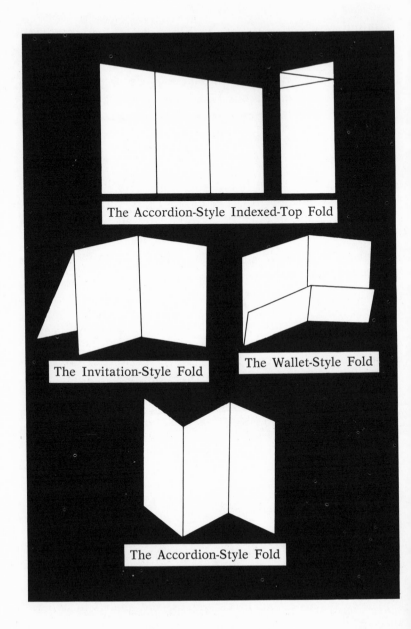

The Accordion-Style Indexed-Top Fold

The Invitation-Style Fold

The Wallet-Style Fold

The Accordion-Style Fold

This cleverly conceived diagonal cut can be handled by any printer's standard paper-cutting equipment. He will charge for the process, but it is a paltry pittance compared to the fancy figures you get hit with once you get involved with die-cutting. The charges they impose can double the cost of a direct-mail piece.

The effect achieved by this simple diagonal slash is to create an instant index—instantly visible at first glance. This makes an ideal presentation for many products or many points.

The Wallet-Style Fold

Department stores are particularly partial to the wallet-style fold, and it's so versatile, you wonder how come no one else has adopted it.

Again it's the plain 8½" by 11" sheet. One off-center vertical fold and two horizontal folds, and you have a wallet, ready to carry a packet of individual little sheets or cards, each featuring a different product or service.

This is the ideal folder to use with the photo envelope described previously. Use a colored paper or a white paper with color ink: "These new models are so beautiful, we felt that only pictures could do them justice." Then fill the inside pockets with miniature catalog sheets of a whole batch of products. Or cards with a picture on front and details on the back.

THE ENVELOPE FOR INSTANT IMPACT

The envelope is not just a carrier of your literature; it is perhaps the most important part of your direct-mail promotion. It is your introduction—the primary attention-getting device on which your promotion can live or die. It takes you to the first vital direct-mail hurdle: getting the buyer to open it now, later, or never.

The #10 envelope is the common garden variety used for all business correspondence. A plain white one of that size is the envelope annually elected to be the most certain-to-be-overlooked envelope on the pile. It guarantees instant obscurity. And if you want to accelerate the movement of a direct-mail piece from desk to wastebasket, just put some lyrical message on the outside like "Come and get big profits now."

With that sort of provocative prose you often save the recipient the nuisance of opening the envelope; he just may toss it out at first glance.

If you must use that kind of white #10 for whatever reason, at least give it a fighting chance. Leave it totally blank so that you are appealing to the prospect's curiosity; he wants to know what's inside—maybe even a price decrease (he can dream, can't he?). Given those odds, he will probably open it.

Squares, oblongs, baronials—these are just some of the more unusual envelopes available as stock items from any envelope house. Ask for a catalog of envelope styles or a list of every size and style that your envelope house carries as stock numbers.

Be sure to convey that you do not wish to be restricted to business-type envelopes. Social styles (the square baronials on rag paper) have a personal look that tempts everyone to open them.

There are many industrial-style envelopes used in factories for carrying interplant communications. There are the bank-style discussed earlier; pay envelopes; small manila envelopes used by jewelers.

Any one of these will stand out on a pile of business correspondence. Try to use a distinctive non-run-of-the-mill style for every promotion. It helps considerably to make that important initial impact.

Sometimes you can pick up stock envelopes in bright

colors. Usually color is a made-to-order job that requires a huge run. But some places have them in stock for special customers. Ask your envelope-supplier. You never know.

There is a stock envelope that has a clear window almost the full size of the envelope (not just a little tiny one for the address). It comes in #10 size and also in a 5" by 8" size. These will display the complete cover of your mailing piece on sight. They create a picture-window effect that has the recipient reading your sales message even before he opens the envelope. What more can you ask of an envelope?

GIANT POSTCARDS— THE TRAVELING BILLBOARDS

No envelopes to fight through. A postcard just hits the desk and spills its story straight out.

It's an instant billboard that cannot be missed. It has to be seen and can be read even as it's being thrown away.

A giant-sized card is a good way to communicate a single fact, a special announcement, a special sale, a new location, a new distributor or warehouse, and so on. Just don't get carried away and start jamming in twelve different things, or you will lose the billboard effect that is the card's only advantage.

HOW TO USE COLOR

Four-color printing is effective but not necessarily four times more effective than one. However, there are instances when full color does a job that really cannot be done with less; when it does not pay to produce the literature at all unless it shows the products in full-color glory.

This is especially true with decorator and fashion merchandise: home furnishings where you feature new designs in smashing new colors; bedspreads; dresses in new fashion fabrics. Or when you are presenting a new colorful line of packaging.

These things cannot be shown properly in black-and-white photography. Words can do so much; they can convey uses, concept, but never colors.

In such situations go for four colors. It really would not pay to go without it. And you don't have to pay all that much to go with it.

Four-Color Bargains

There are specialized printers throughout the country who do four-color printing at almost two-color prices. There must be a catch or two—and there are. But you can probably live with them.

These printers can offer the lower prices because they wait to "gang" a batch of orders and then run them all together on one huge press. That means you get the economy of splitting the cost of a four-color press run with a bunch of other guys.

It's sort of like a charter airplane flight: You cut your expense by sharing the facility but must give up certain luxuries and accommodations.

Like time. You have to wait until the printer accumulates enough jobs to fill his press, so your delivery time can be anywhere from four to eight weeks. Which means if you have an imminent firm deadline, forget it. Try next time when you can plan far ahead and can be elastic about delivery dates.

Like perfect color-matching. Since the printer is trying to please everybody on the press, he cannot give you the custom service of adjusting his ink mixtures to give you exact color. The orange may be a little redder than you'd like, or a bit more yellow. The red may have a slightly purple tinge that is not entirely accurate. They do try to please everyone, and the results are usually pretty fair. It's still four-color and looks beautiful. But if your entire promotion is contingent upon depicting true colors, this method may not be for you. Say, when you are introducing a new hue of blue fabric and a shade off can kill it. Or you are showing a line of imported foods where a slight green cast to the pâté can look like you are selling salmonella. In other words, if absolutely faithful color is vital, skip this printing method. You are better off saving your pennies for a custom run or going to black-and-white photography.

Like quantity. They usually have preset quantity breakdowns; 2,500, 5,000, 10,000, and 25,000 are the standard. It isn't too much of a difficulty to go along with this stipulation; you can usually adjust your needs to the closest prescribed quantity.

Like size. As a rule, 8″ by 10″ and 3″ by 5″ postcards are the only sizes available. If you need anything larger, you're on your own.

These may sound like an inordinate number of limitations, but they're fairly minor restrictions that should not be hard to live with. And if you need four color and cannot afford it any other way, it's well worth the compromises. It won't look like a *National Geographic* cover, but it will sell.

Three Colors for the Price of Two

There's one basic difference between the big-budget advertising field and the small-budget advertising field: They spend all their time devising clever ways to spend money, and we spend all our time figuring ingenious ways to save it.

Consequently, we learn to investigate and observe every process involved in the services we purchase so that we can take full advantage of every potential they offer. That's how this three-color-for-the-price-of-two came about.

Printing charges are determined by many factors: size, paper, quantity, and number of colors used. Each color requires a run through the press. So the more colors, the more runs, the more money.

"But isn't each side of the sheet run separately?" we asked the printer. "Why not change the ink when you change the sides? In other words, print black with red on the front, and then change to black with green on the back." He couldn't see a reason in the world why this couldn't be done, except that he'd have to wash the red ink from the press before the switch to green. But since the charge for a press wash-up is only twenty-five dollars, that was no big deal.

As a result, we came out with a folder that was three colors, at a price just a bit higher than for two! It's a technique that offers a wide versatility of design possibilities, and we have been using it ever since. Try it.

Two-Color Effect for One-Color Price

Do you know why the Chinese are reputed to have become the greatest cooks in the world? Because for centuries they were so bone poor that they had to seek creative, versatile ways to cook with what minimal resources they had.

This may be an apocryphal answer, but it makes a handy illustration of how limited budgets lead to endless creativity. Of which the color printing on color stock is another example.

You know about black ink on white paper; that's rock bottom on the printing price scale. But how about blue ink on tan paper or green ink on gray or maroon ink on blue or brown ink on tan?

It's amazing how many color effects can be achieved

with just the two elements of one color ink and one color paper. Black is usually the preferred color ink for printing halftones (photographs), since it has the proper strength for bringing out detail. But a dark-color ink, with a density that approaches that of black, can often produce a highly acceptable halftone. And look at the variations you can create.

This is particularly important when you are turning out a newsletter or bulletin of any sort that is distributed monthly. It can get pretty boring in straight black and white, and after a while your mailings will be getting a "ho-hum" welcome that means instant wastebasket.

So doodle around with papers and inks, and see what interesting combinations you come up with. You can make each month's mailing look totally different and still pay for only one-color printing!

PLAY WITH PAPER

Paper—or stock, as it's referred to in printing—comes in a tremendous variety of colors, weights, and finishes.

Printers often buy odd lots of unusual papers or have some around from overruns on jobs. Chances are you can get these distinctive papers at regular prices under these circumstances.

Ask your printer what sorts of outstanding or different stock he has on hand. You can achieve some stunning effects that way at no higher cost.

GRAB HIM BY THE EGO

No one can resist a test of his mental ability. Secretly (or not so secretly, as the case may be) every man believes that he is smarter than the men running the country. He is probably right.

Attach a quiz to your direct mail, and the response will

floor you. It's a delightfully sneaky way to lure recipients into reading your material.

You can use a standard puzzle, the professionally prepared jobs that you find in books. Or create a test-yourself quiz: "Biz Quiz. Test your reading ability and powers of observation." Now what living, breathing, egoistical human being could resist that challenge? Then give them a rating system so they can reward themselves with the exhilarating proof of their superior brainpower: "Give yourself 20 points for each correct answer; 80—above average; 90—extraordinary; 100—genius."

The beauty part is that if you base the questions on the facts covered in your direct-mail material, you will be forcing them to read everything carefully. What greater prize could you ask for?

And speaking of prizes, that's not a bad idea, either.

We once offered a prize for the right quiz answers in a mailer and drew a response that nearly paralyzed the shipping room. Again it was that old appeal-to-the-ego gambit, only this enabled them to show off their successes to their children:

"Here's a little gift for you, son."

"Gosh, Dad, where did you get it?"

"Oh, I won it in a quiz."

The answers we sought were based on finding ten mistakes that had been deliberately hidden among the paragraphs of product prose. Anyone who found at least five errors was awarded a Halloween mask for his kids. The results were phenomenal, and we discovered ten more mistakes that were not intentional!

REPETITION—PULL THE COLOR SWITCH

By the time a direct-mail piece goes out, chances are you are sick of it. After all, you've worked on it and seen it so often that you never want to look at it again.

But the guys on your mailing list have seen it only once (if you're lucky). What's to stop you from reprinting the piece at a later date and mailing it again? And maybe even a third time?

Change the colors, and it will look like an entirely different piece. That's a trick that can save you a fortune. You will be able to amortize the basic expenditure of art and copy. Printing is cheaper, too, because printing negatives already exist.

Different colors, maybe different paper—and even you might not recognize it. This is a wonderful way to stretch your ad budget and get more mileage out of your direct-mail expenditures.

THE HOUSE ORGAN

House organs, if you're not familiar with them, are instruments for the virtuoso display of corporate humility.

It is usually a folksy communiqué from the home office in the form of a newsletter or miniature newspaper. In large companies it is used to spread the corporate gospel and gossip among its far-flung personnel and people who have a relationship to the company.

A classic example is the newspaper the telephone company includes in its bills, a cute little chatty gazette filled with human-interest tales of heroism performed by phone-company personnel and other episodes that demonstrate the corporation's vital importance in your life.

It's a great device for speaking about the unspeakable —those generalities of corporate excellence, good service, better-quality merchandise that are impossible to say outright without sounding like the president's mother. It's a device that small companies can use to tremendous advantage.

Everyone boils at the competitor who knocks off a product, manufactures it in his garage, and then peddles it at cut prices. That's the toughest thing to fight in business. You don't want to give him the promotional boost of making a big public statement about the dangers of dealing with Sleazy Sam, nor does it warrant the expense of a mailing. Then how can you warn your customers of the hazards of buying cut-quality merchandise? That's where the house organ comes in.

Slipped in among all the newsy tidbits can be a note about the risks of buying bargains, maybe a case history of some disaster that resulted from someone in the industry buying from shady, shoddy suppliers. No names, please—just subtle hints.

Maybe you have a specialized product or service that appeals to a limited market. It is not worth a full-scale mailing, but you want your customers to know it exists. You can feature it in the pages of the house organ.

Or you have some "slow movers" that you hate to drop from the line; they are profitable, and people do ask for them from time to time. You can show them in the pages of the house organ.

You have a shipping problem; customers are returning merchandise without asking permission, and you are getting stuck with a lot of unwanted, unsalable items. Mention the difficulty in the house organ.

Just think of all the things you would like to tell your customers, censor some of them, and put the rest into your house organ.

It's also a great way to solicit business subtly. Send a regular house-organ mailing to a list of prospects. It keeps your name before them, helps your image (if they enjoy the publication), and reminds them to call upon you next time they need whatever it is you sell.

The house organ, in effect, is a little newspaper in which you are the sole advertiser. Its primary aim is to build readership, to be entertaining and of value to the reader.

Create a name, usually some sort of play on your company name, have a masthead designed, and plan to mail on a fairly regular basis. It should become something your mailing list becomes familiar with and, hopefully, looks forward to.

Now the contents. Current news stories or government edicts that are of interest to the group of readers you are mailing to, with some suitable comment from you. Little anecdotes or jokes are a particularly good idea and assure an extended, maybe permanent life for your paper. Most people have a lousy memory for jokes and tend to hold on to publications that contain them.

And now the commercials. Sprinkled casually through the pages can be your propaganda, casual plugs for your products or services. Don't hit them over the head with these messages, though; weave them gently and introduce them pertinently among the other material. The effect is subtle and stronger.

Here are some examples of how you can lead into these messages.

CAUTION ABOUT CUT-PRICED COMPETITION

A dinner guest at Groucho Marx's house was very puzzled when he examined the sausage put on his plate.

"But this is queer," he said. "One end is bread crumbs!"

"That's right," said Groucho, "in times like these, nobody can make both ends meat!"

*   *   *

It's commendable to cut corners in the kitchen, but it's downright dishonest to do so in business. Unfortunately, a few not-so-scrupulous manufacturers in the field are doing just that by selling off-weight packages.

This may not be the most hilarious of jokes, but it does smooth the way to an attack on your competition.

KEEPING YOUR CORPORATE PROMISES

A ten-year-old boy had a bad habit of swearing. To cure him, his father offered to get him a pet rabbit if he promised to stop swearing. The youngster kept his promise faithfully, and after a month his father brought him a rabbit. Excited with his new pet, he picked her up, and at that exact moment the rabbit proceeded to give birth to an enormous litter. The boy dropped the mother rabbit in horror and cried: "Son of a bitch! The damn thing is falling apart!"

*   *   *

Some promises are pretty tough to keep. But we made a promise when we started in business thirty years ago to make only the highest-quality products. And we have never broken that promise.

These are just some ways to illustrate how the light touch can enable you to make some pretty heavy statements.

The house organ must look like an appealing, easy-to-read newspaper. The size could be anything—from 5" by 8" up to 24" by 18". It should be one color ink on white or colored paper. It should have a standard format. Familiarity is important, and maintaining a consistent format builds recognition.

And very important: Liven up the pages with illustrations—photographs of people, products, or places. Cartoons, drawings. Some art to break up the pattern of words.

Where can you get this art? Get yourself a booklet of

stock art. This is a collection of all kinds of ready-to-use cartoons and drawings in every category. Men, women, children, holidays, occupations, and dozens of others. These are all ready to cut out, paste in, and print from. (Harry Volk Studio, Pleasantville, New Jersey, has a good collection.)

CHAPTER 6

PUBLIC RELATIONS

They used to call them press agents or publicity agents. If you remember the 1940's movies, you'll recognize the type: brash, glib, cocky, and not too couth—ready to pull any stunt to make the papers. Fly to Iceland to sell refrigerators to the Eskimos or to India to offer soap flakes to the women washing dhotis in the Ganges.

"I don't care what you say about my client, as long as you spell his name right!"

Then, somewhere along the way, they turned respectable and got religion. Now they're college-trained in communications; they speak softly and write forcefully. The publicity trade has become the estimable profession called public relations—a most powerful force in government, industry, and education.

Today, when you say public relations—or P.R., as it's commonly referred to—you can mean anything from new-product releases to handling lobbying campaigns in Washington; in short, any area of communications that can reflect on the public image of the corporation.

P.R. SERVES THE MEDIA

A good part of every newspaper and magazine you read is composed of information received from public-relations writers. There's no illicit dealing, no subterfuge. It is based on a mutually beneficial relationship between the editors and the P.R. people.

An editor or columnist depends on information. Years ago, when industry was concentrated in a few urban areas, the writer used to do his own legwork and spadework. But today industry has sprawled into remote hamlets throughout the country and now produces thousands of technologically newsworthy developments every month. It would be virtually impossible for a writer to cover all those beats. So he must depend on reports that come in to him from the companies themselves and their P.R. representatives.

And the term "depend on" means just that. Since the editor cannot check on the accuracy of every news release that comes across his desk, he must rely on the absolute veracity of his sources. This is why P.R. people will speak confidently about their editorial "contacts." There is no mystique involved in developing these relationships; all you have to do is prove to the editors that they can depend on you for honest, factual, well-written news stories, and they will happily accept your news releases. You are, in effect, making their jobs easier, and who doesn't look for that?

Once you know how to prepare and produce a well-organized professional news release—and it isn't difficult —you can issue them to the media as new developments occur, and you will soon develop your own editorial contacts.

HOW TO PREPARE A NEWS RELEASE

Suppose a wicked king ordered you executed but permitted you a last-minute plea for your life, providing your presentation was interesting and entertaining. But as soon as you lost his attention, you lost your head.

You would pour out all your vital facts and most convincing arguments fast, right? You wouldn't save any goodies for later, because there might not *be* a later.

That's just the way you must think when writing a news release. The editor had better know the major points of your story immediately, or you'll lose your audience; ramble, and he'll stop reading. A properly written news release, just like a newspaper story, has all the salient points up front. The substantive facts, the descriptive detailing, the minor points, come along later.

You are fighting a battle to capture his interest and hold it, and the moment you become impalpable and imprecise, the second you go into hyperbole and overstatement, you've lost.

1. Who, What, When, Where, and How

The prime rule in journalism is that the opening paragraph of a news article must contain the answers to these five questions: Who? What? When? Where? and How? The assumption is that the reader may never get past that first paragraph, and you want to be sure that he gets all the facts before he takes off.

This is exactly how you must set up your news releases. Bear in mind that the editor will have to convert your release into a news article. Contrary to popular conception, editors are human and endowed with the same qualities of sloth as the rest of we mortals. The less rewrite work you give him and the closer you adhere to proper journalism form, the greater your chances that he'll use your material intact.

2. Make It News—Not Advertising

No one is kidding anyone else. The editor knows you have prepared the P.R. story for the benefit of your company. But he will print it if the news offers benefit to his readers, if it contains straight facts and no unsubstantiated allegations.

He will not include any advertising adjectives or any statements to the effect that yours is the greatest or any claims that put him in the position of endorsing your company.

You must consider your story as a news article, slanted from the point of view of the readers—what it does for them and how it does it. And skip the superlatives; they'll only get slashed or if too overdone, may get the whole story scratched.

The release should be neatly typed, doubled-spaced, on company letterhead. The words "For Immediate Release" should appear in the upper right-hand corner. This tells the editor that the news is ready to break now. If the happening-date will be sometime hence, say so: "For Release on June 15."

But whatever you do, never misrepresent facts or timing. If you advise an editor that your product or service offers specific features and will be available for sale on a specified date, it damned well better be so, or you'll be on his death list forever.

Every editor worth his salt guards his reputation for accuracy with an intimidating ferocity. And well he should; his integrity is his livelihood. If he tells his readers that something is, and then it isn't, then he soon isn't either.

He may want to check certain details or ask some questions or want some further elaboration on the facts you have provided. Let him know whom to contact, and make it easy by putting your name and phone number at the bottom of the release.

3. Pictures Speak Louder

Always send a photograph with your release if at all possible. It provides more interest to the story and gets you more space in the media.

If it's a product shot, a picture of new packaging, or a new display, you want a simple, vertical shot. No arty lighting—just good sharp, contrasty, nuts-and-bolts stuff. The vertical shot seems to fit in better with the editorial makeup of special columns in magazines. For instance, the new-products sections of almost every magazine accept only vertical shots.

Here is a special money-saving tip. Send 5″ by 7″ photo prints with your publicity releases; it can cut your photo print expense and reduce mailing costs considerably. When you get your 8″ by 10″ original photograph from the photographer, send it to a photo-copying company and have them make a 5″ by 7″ copy negative, from which they will make as many 5″ by 7″ copy prints as you need. There's no need to send out the larger 8″ by 10″ prints; the 5″ by 7″ is just as effective and is completely acceptable by all publications.

When mailing photos, don't forget to insert a cardboard stiffener in the envelope. One crease or crack, and your picture is unusable. And if you've ever seen the manner in which the post office handles mail, you realize that photographs need all the protection they can get.

WHAT SHOULD BE PUBLICIZED

There are some trade magazines that will happily publish the hot story that your truck bays have been repainted.

Either they are so pressed for news to fill their pages that they will print anything remotely resembling news or they are so hard up for revenue that they will print any item that might flatter you enough to induce you to toss some advertising bucks their way.

But the better publications have specific standards for newsworthy material. Here are the most popular types of stories that are considered acceptable by all media.

The New (or Improved) Product or Service

Every magazine has a new-products section, and it's usually the first and best read part of the book. When you have a new product or service or have added some improvements or innovations to an old one, that warrants a story.

For example, suppose you had just arranged to import a new line of riding hats.

NEW SAFER HUNTING CAP BY WATERFORD
An English hunt cap that insures rider safety with a fiber-glass inner shell has been introduced this week by Waterford Ridingwear Ltd., Waterford, New Jersey.

Notice that the main point is in the heading, with the word "new" prominent, and that the points that make it new and newsworthy are completely covered in the opening line. (What? How? When? Who? and Where? are answered.) Then follow with all the details of construction, colors, sizes, and prices.

The Grand Opening

A new plant, new wing, new store, new offices, new branch, even refurbished quarters, can be developed into a newsworthy event with a little color and style. Make a big-deal occasion of it. Hire a photographer, set a date, and invite some V.I.P.'s. Local officials are the first choice. They're easy—just tell them a photographer will be there, and they'll show up beaming bonhomie.

If you are a distributor or a retailer, invite executives of supplier organizations. The more V.I.P.'s you have, the more space the magazine will give your story.

You might spring for some booze and nibbles and then invite the trade-magazine editorial staffs. The press is renowned for their inability to resist a freebie blast, and you usually end up with good coverage and much goodwill that can pay dividends in future P.R. acceptances. After the festivities are over, you will have the basis of an excellent news release. It might run something like this:

VIE & VIN LTD. OPENS NEW WAREHOUSE

Vie & Vin Ltd., Englewood, New Jersey, importers of French wines, celebrated the opening of their new warehouse on June 27, attended by the mayor of Englewood and members of the French consulate.

The new warehouse will streamline and extend production facilities to an estimated doubling of capability.

Etc., etc.

You would then complete the release with details of who was there and what future growth and successes the new facility will achieve.

The accompanying photo should show all the company principals, plus as many dignitaries as you can fit in. If your photographer knows his stuff, he will be sure to pose everyone holding identifiable samples of the company products, preferably against a background that shows the company name. And when you send out the photos, be sure you attach a caption properly identifying the persons shown.

A New Display or New Packaging

You have repackaged your line or have created a new store display. This warrants publicity. Treat it much as you would a new-product story, and include a photograph, of course.

Packaging magazines are particularly receptive to publicity on interesting packages and displays. If your new design has any innovative aspects or is graphically impressive, send the release to the packaging media as well as to your usual trade publications.

A New Executive, a New Distributor, a Corporate Promotion

Here you want a straightforward story that should be accompanied by a recent portrait of the individual. (Don't send a ten-year-old picture, much as the fellow concerned favors the more flattering rendition. When he gets around to the customers, they're likely to think his few months on the job have aged him rapidly.)

The release should include who he is, what he will be doing, what he is expected to accomplish (here's where you slip in the corporate commercial about specific areas of sales activities), and details of his education, experience, and family. Don't forget the local newspapers. The business pages of the newspapers in the town where he lives and the city where the company is located will gladly include the item.

A New Advertising-Promotion Campaign

An unusual advertising and sales-promotion campaign affords two opportunities for publicity—before and after.

A preview-of-the-campaign release would cover the elements, plans, and projected media scheduled for the program. You could photograph some of the components and collateral material and send it with the release.

An aftermath story would be concerned with the great successes achieved and any specific sales results or human-interest ramifications.

For example, Redactron Corporation, who makes an editing typewriter, ran a "Free the Secretary" campaign that was aimed at the bright secretaries who bridle at the boredom of incessant typing and retyping. Centered around an ad headed, "The Death of the Dead-End Secretary," which ran in *Ms., New York, New Woman,* and *The Secretary* magazines, it offered buttons, streamers, and memo pads saying "Free the Secretary," pointing up how the editing typewriter could take over the drudgery of repetitive typing and free the secretary for more challenging chores.

The campaign struck a contemporary nerve and generated an outpouring of interesting correspondence from secretaries and executives throughout the country. The reaction was so intense and enthusiastic that it became the basis of a success-story publicity release that was printed by all pertinent media. This kind of story is of interest to the advertising and sales-promotion publications, as well as to the advertising columns of many newspapers.

A New Catalog

Most magazines have a column devoted to the description of new literature available to their readers. If you have any new booklet, pamphlet, or catalog that would be of interest to the readers of specific publications and more important, whose interest could be of benefit to you, shoot out a release on it. Include a description of its aims, contents, and potential value to the readers. And if it is sufficiently prepossessing, send a photo of it.

HOW TO USE P.R. TO OPEN NEW MARKETS

Would you ever think of selling pillowcases in beauty salons? Or knocked-down versions of a lamp in hobby shops?

But they do sell—and very well, too.

Sometimes the most way-out outlets for products turn out to be fantastically fruitful. The problem is: How do you uncover these hidden sales sources easily and inexpensively?

Answer: with a little imagination, P.R., and a *Bacon's Publicity Checker.*

Just as the guidebook of the advertising-media departments is *Standard Rate & Data*, the indispensable reference guide of the public-relations departments is *Bacon's Publicity Checker*, available from H. R. Bacon and Company, 14 East Jackson Boulevard, Chicago, Illinois 60605. This handy little volume lists every magazine and periodical in the United States and Canada according to category. It furnishes names, addresses, other important information involving the selectivity of acceptable material.

Go through *Bacon's*, and look for potential sales areas for your products. You will come across markets you never dreamed existed in cohesive sales-approachable form. Be daring. Send new-product releases to the publications of every possible market that could remotely be interested. You may get responses from totally unexpected areas and open up brand-new sales outlets never before tapped.

For instance, did you know that hairdressers sell the most variegated variety of non-hair-connected products— from underwear to umbrellas? And that this lucrative market can be easily reached via a group of beauty supply companies who have sales forces soliciting salons on a steady, volume-selling basis? The pillowcase-manufacturer discovered that satin pillowcases, which ladies use to preserve the states of their costly coiffures while slumbering, made a great packaged item for salon sales.

And the knocked-down lamps. Have you ever tried to assemble assorted equipment that arrived with English instructions illiterately translated from the original Yugoslavian? Then it may be incomprehensible to you that anyone would actually enjoy that sort of work. But one man's horror is another man's hobby. If you make any type of equipment, you might think of packaging a product in a somewhat unassembled form, calling it a kit, and selling it through hobby shops. (Of course, don't pack it in too primitive a form. The rule is that it must be able to be assembled with the ordinary home tools. And that does not normally include a drill press or a trip-hammer.)

Be imaginative. Be intrepid. After all, how much will the whole fishing expedition cost? With P.R. you can afford to indulge in the most exotic marketing exploration sorties. And who knows, you may uncover a million-dollar market that had been totally overlooked!

HOW TO MAKE NEWS WHEN NOTHING IS HAPPENING

A good P.R. firm doesn't hang around waiting for exciting developments—they make them. In fact, if you should retain a P.R. organization and then find that they're calling constantly to ask what's new, unretain them. They're not doing their job.

You can produce newsworthy articles in many ways. Here are just a few suggestions.

The Prediction

One of the simplest bases for a nonhappening news release is the prediction from the president of the company.

This is the standard headline-grabbing technique of clothing-designers. Remember the chap who hit all the media a few years ago with the prediction that within five years women would be wearing topless bathing suits?

We picked up considerable linage in newspapers throughout the country with a release that read, "A Soda Fountain in Every Home?" and predicted that homes of the future would have built-in soda systems. Of course, the quoted individual was described as the president of such-and-such a company—and there's the commercial plug.

This sort of approach takes some ingenuity and imagination, but think on it.

Suppose you ran an employment agency. You could issue a story headed, "Hiring by computers seen in 1982," and go on into a statement by the president of the agency foretelling the existence of a city-wide central employment computer bank that listed every job and available applicant.

These are just some suggestions. But as you can see, it's not too difficult to come up with newsworthy predictions. The secret of the technique is to make a statement that is intriguing, maybe even fantastic, but never incredible.

What this technique accomplishes is to endow the quoted person with instant expertise. He has made a publicized prediction; ergo, he is a revered seer. Who wouldn't want to deal with a company headed by such a knowledgeable, respected man?

The State of the Economy

Another device to break into the news media is to have the president of the company come out with a statement about the condition of the economy. It's good, but it may get worse; it's bad, but it will get better. Of course, you must back this up with a few accurate statistics, and those are easily obtained from government agencies, not to mention the daily newspapers.

The Famous User

Nothing gets the consumer more than the sight of a celebrity enjoying your product. You don't have to pay fancy testimonial fees, either. The famous can be surprisingly cooperative—and chintzy.

Keep your ears and eyes open. At some point you will hear of some renowned person who uses your product or service. Write to him or her with an offer for free merchandise in exchange for permission to photograph him with your product.

Sounds wild, right? After all, with all the money they rake in, why should they bother with barter? But I've done it a number of times; something for nothing appeals to everyone.

Many years ago, when Yul Brynner was starring on Broadway in *The King and I*, my secretary excitedly showed me a request from him for a booklet on photo albums offered in our ads. What could I lose? I wrote him and made the barter offer.

Guess what? Two weeks later the photographer and I were backstage at *The King and I*, clicking away at the star—in full costume, yet—obligingly holding our albums. Armed with written permission to use the photographs in our promotion, we left him with about a hundred dollars' worth of albums (cost: twenty-five dollars).

The Specialized Application

How your product is or can be used, and by whom, can get you space in diversified media you never dreamed of reaching.

For example, you manufacture a lamp. It could be a wonderful piano light. It would be handy on a sewing machine. It's ideal for home needleworkers. It's the perfect light to apply cosmetics by. Philatelists and numismatists (stamp and coin collectors in plain English) would appreciate its strong direct light.

Here's how you get coverage in music publications, home handicraft publications, stamp- and coin-collecting publications, women's pages, and beauty hint columns.

You hire a model for the day. Of if you have some particularly photogenic daughters or employees around, they'll do fine. Then find a well-furnished home that has a piano and sewing machine. Some member of the firm is sure to volunteer his or her place. Nearly everyone is flattered that you rate his home highly enough to want to use it for photographed room settings. Then you bring in your photographer, on a daily location rate (usually about a few hundred dollars), and shoot the lamp in use in all possible situations and settings. A smoothly run effort should yield anywhere from twelve to twenty shots.

Then write one basic release that describes the prime construction features of the lamp, its colors, styles, and price, and where available.

Now tailor that one basic release to a series of media with a different heading and opening paragraph, each slanted to appeal to one specific market. For example, the piano picture would go with a release headed, "A Note on Lighting," and be followed by "A new lamp that was especially designed to follow the musician instead of just 'go with' the piano has been introduced by . . . ."

The home handicraft picture might be accompanied with a release that read, "Eye-Light of the Year for Close Work," and then lead into an opening paragraph that indicated that the lamp was designed especially for the needs of people who did needlework, crewelwork, and so on.

From that one day's shooting and one basic release you should generate enough P.R. possibilities to get you into dozens of publications. Use your *Bacon's Checker* for the editors' names and addresses—and mail. Then sit back and wait for the clippings and inquiries to come in.

SUNDRY P.R. SUGGESTIONS

Bacon's and many other P.R. mailing services will handle the whole thing for you. Just give them an original release and photograph, indicate which category of publications you want to hit (use *Bacon's* numbers), and they'll take care of the rest. They reprint the release and photograph in the desired quantity and mail to whomever you select. It's unbelievably easy—and effective.

Every industry is loaded with trade shows. There are certain fields where there are between fifty and a hundred exhibits a year. Sometimes they are small hotel shows put on by a local group, sometimes larger efforts by national organizations. But one thing they all have in common is the need for P.R.

Get a list of all the shows in which your firm plans to participate, and then send off the following letter to the executive director of each:

> Dear Sir:
>
> Can we supply you with exhibitor information, photos, etc., on the XYZ Company's products for this year's show? We'd like to be sure that we are included in the press kit, for example, and would welcome any suggestions you might have.
>
> If this is outside your activities, would you kindly let us know the person or organization handling promotion for the show?

You can achieve a fair amount of success and press

coverage with this do-it-yourself method of P.R. But it takes a lot of time and steady commitment to really do the job properly.

If you can afford to retain an outside P.R. firm, do. Good ones are available at rates that range from five hundred dollars a month all the way up into the thousands. The rate you arrive at is determined by how intense a coverage you need and what you can afford. Let them give you proposals of what they feel they can do within the restricted guidelines you have stipulated. Don't be snowed by a fast talker with glib promises of the cover of *Newsweek*. Ask to see what they have done for others and how long they have been associated with the accounts they handle.

Avoid the "revolving door" operations so prevalent among some large national and internationally operating P.R. firms. The name describes the in and out movement of disenchanted clients—usually because of long promises and short shrift. Many of these outfits send in their big guns to secure the account and then turn you over to rank neophytes or the itinerant juniors who move around from firm to firm to build an impressive résumé.

For a small business with a small budget, your best bet is a small shop whose principals will give you skilled attention and where your account is important.

CHAPTER 7

VISUAL SALES PRESENTATIONS

If you have ever sold (and everyone has, whether it be a product, a service, an idea, or oneself), have you ever found yourself saying, in the course of the sales pitch, "Now, what I should've mentioned earlier . . ."?

Have you ever interrupted yourself with a phrase like "Here's something I want to show you" and then started searching your pockets and attaché case for a letter, a folder, or some other pertinent item only to find when you finally dug it out that (1) it's slightly crushed and very coffee-stained and (2) the prospect and you have lost the whole flow of your argument while you were on your little hunt?

Well, this can never happen when you use a visual presentation. All your facts are marshaled in advance, neatly prearranged in the correct sequence to lead you straight to getting the order.

A visual presentation is a simplified, illustrated version of your sales story that you show as you give your sales talk. Just like a television commercial, it's a planned combination of words, pictures, and sound which hits the prospect's eye and ear simultaneously, thus convincing him faster, surer.

This modern sales tool has proven so effective that today all large companies equip their sales forces with visuals prepared at great expense by professional sales-presentation experts. There is no reason why your sales force should not have the benefit of this same proven sales-building weapon.

This is another area where expensive does not mean more efficient. It's not the elaborate artwork that makes it effective, but the proper analysis and organization of your selling story. And it could be in a two-dollar store-bought binder or a twenty-dollar custom job—the impact is the same.

I will show you quite simply how to prepare a visual sales presentation that can, without question, improve the sales performance of every person in your company who uses it.

HOW TO PREPARE A BUDGET-VERSION VISUAL PRESENTATION

You will need the following equipment:

1. An 8½″ by 11″ ring binder with plastic sheet-protectors. If you can get an easel style, so much the better. The easel has the advantage of standing to give the prospect a better viewing angle.

2. Heavy white paper sheets (about twelve). On these you will paste your illustrations and write your headlines. These will be the finished pages of your presentation that will be slipped into plastic sheet-protectors of the ring binder.

3. Tissue sheets (about twelve). These can be onionskin and will be used for roughing out the presentation.

4. Felt-tipped pens: black, red, blue, and any other

colors you like. These will be used for writing and decoration.

5. A ruler, a sheet of graph paper, rubber cement.

The actual pasting-in is the easiest and last part of your preparation. The first and most important part is planning and arranging it. Here are the seven steps you will follow:

1. Analyze your product or service, and list all the reasons why the prospect should buy.

2. Arrange these reasons in proper order.

3. Make a list of all the points that support and prove each reason.

4. Condense the reasons and proof into headlines and captions.

5. Gather illustrations for your visual presentation.

6. Make a rough page-by-page layout.

7. Paste up and print the actual presentation.

Now let's take these steps one at a time.

1. List all the reasons why the prospect should buy. Include every possible reason you can think of. You can always cut down later.

For instance, if you sell industrial equipment or components, your list might include: it produces a lot of units; the company has a good reputation, is growing; product lasts a long time; maintenance is simple; it's easy and inexpensive to install; insurance rates are low; prospect knows of other plants that are satisfied with the product.

If you sell an item for resale to retailers or wholesalers, your list might include: faster turnover; big profit margin; good volume sales; creates more store traffic; big demand for this type of product; product guaranteed and backed by excellent company reputation; company's vigorous advertising and sales promotion.

If you sell directly to consumers, you might list: product offers convenience and comfort; improves health; assures safety; saves money; adds beauty; lends prestige.

If you solicit funds or memberships for organizations, your list might include: past activities of the group; evils they have corrected; improvements they have initiated; their work has added value to property; who supports it and who opposes it.

2. *Arrange these reasons in proper order.* Put them in order of importance to prospect so that they build up and lead directly into your asking the prospect to act.

3. *Make a list of all the points that support and prove each reason.* Okay, you have a convincing list of "reasons to buy." But at this point they're merely statements. Now let's take them up one by one and see what we might say further to prove them.

For instance, if you are selling a piece of equipment, you probably have a heading that says, "It's easy to install." Okay, why? You might elaborate by saying: "It takes only three hours to set it up. Unskilled plant labor can do the job. No special wires, ducts, pipes, etc., are needed."

Or if you sell an item for resale, you probably have a "reason to buy" that says, "You get a fast sales turnover." Your proof of that statement might be: "Colorful, smart package stimulates impulse sales. Low retail price attracts more customers. Heavy advertising campaign presells."

And so on. After you have listed facts that prove each of your "reasons to buy," your story is pretty well set. Now we're ready to start converting it into a visual sales presentation.

4. *Condense the reasons and proof into headlines and captions.*

Ever notice the headline above every item in your daily newspaper—the way it summarizes in "shorthand" what appears in the body of the article? That's what you will do now. It's really quite easy. Going back to the salesman of equipment and his first "reason to buy" that dealt with ease and economy of installation, our headline for that page could be "LOW INSTALLATION COSTS." Our subheads would be condensed to read:

Quickly Assembled
Plant Labor
No Alterations

And for the salesman whose products are sold for resale and his "reasons to buy" concern sales turnover, our headline and subheads for that page might read:

FAST SALES TURNOVER
Eye-Stopping Package
Attractively Priced
Presold by Advertising

Your heading should never be too specific, or there will be nothing left for you to say. Just remember that you will be right there to elaborate on each point.

5. Gather illustrations for your visual presentation.

Here's where you decide what you're going to use or make up to illustrate each of your selling points. Look over your "reasons to buy," and try to think of what sort of illustration would best emphasize each point.

You can use photographs or drawings cut from your company catalogs, bulletins, or ads. Good sources for appropriate pictures are your trade publications. Or even general magazines. Just go through them, and you'll get plenty of ideas. For instance, if you want to illustrate that your product has strength, you might clip out a picture of a bulldozer or a strong-looking muscle man. If you want to point up the fact that your product is flame-resistant, you might clip out a picture of a fire from a newspaper, then put a big X through it to illustrate that this cannot happen.

Use graphs to show records over a period of time, or growth in sales or markets can easily be shown via graphs that you can make yourself. Cut off as big a piece as you need, and make a simple graph like this, using your colored pen to make the curve.

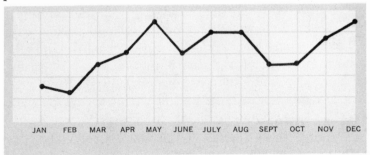

Use bar charts to sharpen comparisons between your product or services and competitive ones. You can place the bars vertically or horizontally. Use one color for your product, another for all other makes. Make your own bar charts easily by using **thick-nib** felt pens or stripes of colored tape.

Every prospect wants to know which companies thought well enough of your product or service to buy it. If a printed list of customers is not available, you can make one by clipping names from their stationery or from ads in magazines. Or you can get a nice artistic effect by typing names and underscoring them in different colors.

6. *Make a rough page-by-page layout.*

Now that all your facts are assembled, you're ready to arrange them, or as the commercial artists call it, to lay it out. Use your tissue sheets for this. Take your elements for each page, and rough them into a neat, well-spaced arrangement.

Note: Use only the right-hand pages of your presentation. We never show anything on the facing left-hand page and feature only one "reason to buy" per page. Why? Because it has been proved that if you put one idea on the left-hand page and a different one on the right-hand page, your presentation loses its punch. What happens is, while you're talking about one point, the prospect's eye roams across to a different one, and you've lost his attention! Sometimes, though, if you have a lot to say about one "reason to buy," you might spread it across two facing pages. Then be sure to run your heading across both pages. But you still permit the prospect to see one "reason to buy" at a time.

OPENING PAGE: This is the page that introduces you and whatever you're selling to the prospect. All it need show is the name of your product plus a picture of it or something representing it. Under the illustration will go a list of all the important "reasons to buy." It is sort of a preview of what you will prove to the prospect inside the presentation; it is a teaser to catch his interest. Just write in your headings and subheadings, and merely place your illustrations in position.

SECOND PAGE: Take your first "reason-to-buy" heading, subheads, and illustrations. For example, you might have a "reason to buy" plus illustrations like this:

LOW INSTALLATION COSTS	(An actual penny which can be pasted right on the page)
Quickly Assembled	(Your own drawing of a clock indicating, say, a three-hour period)

Plant Labor   (Group of workmen or a man at
                           work, clipped from magazine)

No Alterations   (Picture of a blueprint with big
                           X drawn through it: "You don't
                           need blueprints.")

Solid, Dependable   (Photo of Rock of Gibraltar
                           clipped out of a Prudential In-
                           surance Company advertisement)

FOLLOWING PAGES: Take the rest of your "reasons to buy,"
and repeat the procedure. If you have a lot to say and show
about one point, make a two-page spread with any two
layouts.

CLOSING PAGE: Here's where you put the all-important
sales closer. If you haven't gotten the order before you
reach this point, this page gives you the cue to ask for the
order now. For instance, you might list the available
models of your product here, which prompts you to take
out your order book and ask, "Which would be the most
convenient for you?" Or you might make this a summary
of all the "reasons to buy," which gives you the cue to say,
"That's why you must buy a . . . ," and ask for the order.

7. *Paste up and print the actual presentation.*

Now that you have all your material arranged, you're
ready to do the finish on the white sheets. Print all your
page headings and all your subheads, but don't let the
word "print" scare you. You can use either of two methods
to achieve a fine effect. If you are using a typewriter, space
the letters out, using all capital letters for main headings
and small letters for subheadings, like this:

LOW INSTALLATION COSTS
Quickly Assembled

If you can letter neatly, by all means do your own printing, aided with the ruler edge. Add color by underscoring, circling, or drawing arrows to various headings and sales points. Now paste everything in place on the white mounting sheets, and insert in plastic sheet-protectors.

Okay, that's it. You now have a well-organized sales presentation that will enable your salesmen to sell more, sell faster, and sell better. Each salesman should have one. But before he uses it, give him the following pointers on how to get the most out of this selling tool.

USING YOUR PRESENTATION EFFECTIVELY

Give the prospect a reason to want to see your visual presentation. Find out about his special interests and problems before you make your call. Then you can get his interest immediately by stating how your product can solve his problems, which leads into your saying, "May I show you how it would work for you?" For instance, you may have learned that the prospect is having problems with high maintenance on competitive industrial equipment. In that case you could begin your call with "We have cut down maintenance expenses for ten companies in your industry. This presentation shows how we can do it for you, too. May I show it to you?" In this way he is more receptive—he wants to see your visual.

Know in advance where you will set up your presentation. Pick an advantageous arrangement for showing your presentation. Ask your prospect to clear his desk if that's best. If there are two prospects, try to keep them on the same side of you.

Don't just read your presentation—show interest and enthusiasm. Read the main headline and subheadings, but put sincere "belief in your products" into your voice.

Use the visual as a stepping stone to describe details.

Here's how you can tailor your visual to each prospect.

Read the headline, which is general, then relate it specifically to the prospect. Use appropriate examples of interest to him.

Handle interruptions casually, and get back on the track. Of course, you must answer the prospect's questions. If the point he raises is vital, answer it at once, even if it means flipping to another page. But if possible, try to handle his question casually with "We'll get to that in a moment."

Make the prospect part of the story. Wherever possible, try to get your prospect into the act. When you show pictures of companies who have used the product a long time, you might say somthing like "Their standing in the industry is pretty much the same as yours, isn't it?" When you show the letterheads or names of the companies who have bought your product, you could say, "Your company belongs in a fine list like this, don't you think?" Whenever you see that a point has touched a subject close to the prospect's heart, and he wants to expand and elaborate on what you've said, let him take over, and you listen. He'll sell himself a lot faster than you will.

Give life and your personality to the visual. The material in each page of your finished presentation is the skin and bones of your story. It's up to you to give it life and personality when using it.

Read the copy printed or typed on the page to the prospect, and then expand the point in your own words. For example, take the opening of a salesman selling industrial equipment. With the presentation open at the opening page, you might say:

"Mr. Jones, I think I can show you how you can save money, lots of money, and really make money with our Excelsior machine. You start enjoying the savings almost from the minute the truck unloads the equipment at your door. Because one of the remarkable features of this machine is"—at this point you turn the page to the "low installation costs" story and keep right on talking—"low installation costs. And you make a saving here, Mr. Jones, in several different ways. In the first place, it is very quickly assembled; it generally takes no more than two or three hours to do the job. You get that machine at your door in the morning, and it's assembled and working for you before the day is done.

"What's more, Mr. Jones, you don't need any graduate engineers to make the installation. It can be done by your own plant labor. Any of these guys [point to the illustration of a group of men at a plant] could do the job—it's so simple. As a matter of fact, if your secretary is handy with a wrench and screwdriver, she could probably do the job while you're taking a long lunch.

"You see, what makes it such a speedy, easy installation is that [point to third caption and illustration] no alterations are needed, as is the case with so many other types of machines. You don't have to install new circuits or new fuel lines or new ducts or new plumbing. You just put it down, plug it in, and put it to work. And when I say, just put it down, that's exactly what I mean.

"This machine [point to the last subhead] requires no bolting. This machine is so beautifully designed, it is so perfectly balanced, that if your floor is level, the machine will be as steady as the Rock of Gibraltar. You don't have any expense of preparing the floor area or anything like that."

You see, the notes on the page give you your cue to take off and develop each argument. Your story stays with him because he has a visual picture of the point you're making before you go on to the next.

Win the prospect's agreement. Try to get him to nod agreement with the arguments you develop. For example, after you've finished your story on low costs, you might say, "These add up to pretty impressive savings even to a company of your size, don't they, Mr. Jones?"

Ask for the order. Never wait till you get to the end of your presentation to ask for the order if there's an opportunity to do so earlier. If you're selling industrial equipment and your first point impresses the prospect strongly, ask for the order as soon as you've made the point. You could say something like "Our ABC model is just about the right size for your plant. Would you want that, or the CBA model which will take care of some expansion?" If you can get him choosing between models, you've made a sale. If you're selling an item for resale and the prospect responds to "profit margin" argument, don't wait to finish the presentation to ask for the order. Ask him, then and there, how many he wants for his initial order.

Keep asking for the order right through the presentation. If you get the order at an early stage, close up the presentation, and take out your order book or contract blank. There's no point in continuing the presentation to "sell" him; there might be something in it later on that might possibly unsell him.

Of course, if no opening seems to appear as you go through the presentation, make sure you ask for the order after you've finished your story. "That's why this will make money for you, Mr. Jones. Now, which model do you want?" or "How many gross shall we ship you?" or "How much of a contribution can we count on from you?"

Know your story perfectly. Practice the "script" that goes with each page. Try the presentation on your family, your friends, your associates in the office. Make sure you have the story pat, but don't tell it as though you were doing a recitation. Make sure you know how to answer or take care of every variety of argument or interruption. Then, go out and sell.

Good hunting—and happy closings.

CHAPTER 8

TRADE SHOWS

A client of ours had a sales manager. At least, they said they did, and there was an office with the man's name and title on the door. But after visiting the company repeatedly over a six-month period and never seeing the man, I began to suspect he was a myth. Until someone told me why he was never there: "He's at shows."

That's one of the dangers of trade shows; you can over-do them.

Years ago every industry had its one big annual show that everyone who was anyone attended. You could be sure that all the important buyers and supplier company brass would be there. Then some smart organizers sniffed the sweet smell of money and started small independent shows all over the place. And then local trade associations decided this was a good way to raise cash and get a piece of the action. And they started small local shows.

And before you knew it, if a sales manager didn't like administrative desk work or found his homelife a drag, he would—with great show of conscientious sacrifice—manage to involve himself and the company in enough trade shows to keep him on the move ten months a year.

Beware of the "overshow" syndrome. And check the motives and qualifications of any sales manager or executive who insists on personally participating in all of them. A lot of the old-timers of the slap-'em-on-the-back and press-the-flesh school overrate the importance of trade shows. It's usually a substitute for the more modern selling techniques that they cannot grasp.

Many small companies have such men who function as sales managers without really fulfilling or even understanding the full ramifications of the job. Often an individual who started as the "outside man" years ago sort of grew into the role of handling sales. They don't really know how to direct a sales force, are totally unfamiliar with scientific sales techniques and motivational methods, and are a severe liability to their company.

But getting back to trade shows. I am not deprecating their importance, because they have a vital place in business. They can be extremely expensive, what with the costs of the space, attending personnel, transportation, and the display structure. That's why it is important to get the most possible value from each show, to develop the most efficacious display for your needs, and to devise ways to attract the most possible traffic in your exhibit. There are four basic kinds of displays: crated, self-contained, prefab, and stock.

THE CRATED UNIT

Crated units can be as simple or as elaborate as you like or can afford. They are made of all sorts of materials —wood, plastic, masonite, etc—and are shipped in a wooden crate (which often costs as much as the display). There's the rub. It's a pain in the neck waiting around at a show to have the crate opened, removed, and brought back when it's time to pack up.

Not to mention the huge ransom extorted by the assorted union-affiliated gentlemen who are designated to handle it. And if you have ever dealt with these gallant chaps, you know that the number of hours you wait for your crate has a direct correlation with the number of bills you pile on their palms. So the crate becomes like a man's hat which must be checked everywhere; it's not the initial cost that gets you—it's the upkeep.

THE SELF-CONTAINED UNIT

Here's how you can avoid the costly crate. The self-contained unit is designed to fold up into itself and become its own shipping container. It is sort of a display on the inside and a crate on the outside.

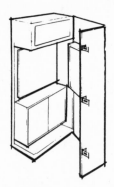 

Self-Crating Unit: No shipping case is needed. The entire display folds into itself, forming its own crate.

This is a most convenient style and can save you hours and dollars. But unfortunately this kind of construction imposes severe design limitations.

THE PREFAB UNIT

Prefab units are the least expensive displays you can get. They are made of corrugated board that has been merged to pegboard.

This sort of display comes knocked down and must be hooked together in a rather tedious way. But the company you buy them from can arrange to have someone at the exhibit site to help set it up.

STOCK DISPLAYS

Many display houses have stock display units that they will customize for you. They will paint your company identification on the header, add lights where you want, and paint the entire display in your choice of colors.

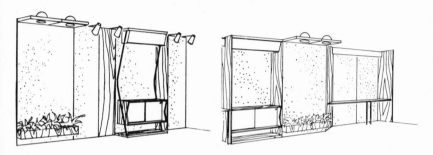

Stock Displays: Design your own exhibit economically by combining stock units to suit your specific needs and size requirements. The panels are usually pegboard. You can often get a ten-foot exhibit for under five hundred dollars.

The stock display can be a very economical solution to the multishow problem. After all, one display cannot be in more than one place at a time. Sometimes there is an overlap in show dates, with one of the shows being of lesser importance. Here it is a good idea to have a less expensive stock unit that you can use for the minor shows.

MODULAR DISPLAYS

If you find you must participate in a number of major shows and each one demands a different-sized exhibit, you need a modular display.

Have the display designed in sections so that you can add and subtract sections to accommodate the varied exhibit spaces.

Of course, you personally will not design whatever unit you choose. But you will direct the professional display firm that you engage and tell them what specific features you want included.

When planning a totally effective show exhibit, there are many other factors besides product display that should be considered.

When given a space to furnish, most people tend to push everything against the walls, leaving the entire inside of the room vacant. This sort of uninspired interior decorating shows a lack of understanding of how furniture should be used to form spatial and traffic patterns.

Don't make that mistake when designing your exhibit. Don't cover the back and sides only, leaving a bare hollow in the middle.

ISLANDS AND COUNTERS

Use islands and counters to get more out of the limited space, make your booth more interesting and inviting-looking, and get more efficient traffic patterns.

A center island coming out at a right angle from the rear wall is very functional. It divides the booth into two selling areas, so that two salesmen can work simultaneously without falling over each other. This island can be a counter, a bookshelf, or any sort of free-standing unit that serves both sides.

A counter or table or island in front of the display, coming at right angles from the sides of the booth, can be your most effective sales-stimulating area. It furnishes a display space at the prime traffic spot—right where it hits the eyes of passersby coming down the aisles. This is a good spot to set up your new product or announcement of any unusual offering.

It can also perform the invaluable function of inviting

potential customers to stop and browse, unhampered by the threat of having to commit themselves to entering the booth.

The hardest thing to accomplish at a show is to lure people in. There are usually so many things to be seen, so many floors to be covered, that visitors are loath to be drawn into any booth other than those of their prime suppliers. You have to do it insidiously—stop them as they pass with a particularly intriguing front-counter presentation. Then as they linger to examine the offering, your salesman has the chance to make his pitch and hopefully provide enough incentive to convince the browser to enter the booth.

CARPETING? COUCHES?

Have you ever walked down trade-show aisles and passed booths where sales personnel were lounging comfortably on couches and chairs, maybe chatting happily with each other? I say "passed booths," because that is what you will usually do when you see such a cozy scene. After all, who wants to be the bad guy who breaks up the party?

This is why I discourage the installation of too-comfortable seating in a trade-show booth. I don't mean to be harsh or unsympathetic to the plight of the people who work trade-show booths. I have done it myself many times and am familiar with the attendant rigors: the stretches of deadly boredom when not a soul turns up for hours, alternated with the frenetic bedlam when suddenly two hundred people start swarming in groups of tens. And always that persistent, pervading aroma of greasy hot dogs and burned coffee.

Of course, seating is needed. But it should be purely functional, not the kind that incurs lounging. Too-comfortable salesmen intimidate people and discourage browsing.

They are loath to disturb the recliners and will frequently pass by rather than intrude.

Also, a comfortable couch encourages visitors to hang around and rest awhile. Now I'm all for hospitality, especially for customers. But once you've taken their orders, who needs them cluttering up the booth?

But carpeting is a good idea. Feet go fast at a show, and you need all the help you can get. The floors are cold and hard and become more so as time goes on. You can usually rent carpeting, or bring your own. And since we discourage sitting, let's at least make standing more comfortable.

DISTRIBUTE LITERATURE, NOT CATALOGS

"Er-er, have you got a catalog?"

That's one of the most-asked idle questions heard at a show and the one that can cost you a fortune in wasted literature.

A person visiting a trade-show booth feels he or she ought to walk away with something. It gives him a sense of accomplishment, as though he has done the correct businesslike thing. After all, he is attending the show to amass trade information, and here he has amassed some— a catalog. And later, when he has the time—back in his office or home or hotel room—he'll look it over and study it carefully.

Uh-huh. Sure he will, if he still has it when he gets there.

Or maybe he has bothered the salesman and bought nothing. People feel less guilty about walking out when they ask for a catalog, thus leaving the salesman with the hope that there may be business forthcoming.

Perhaps his intentions are strong, but unfortunately his arms get weak. After accumulating catalogs and other sundry literature from booth after booth, lugging the sack of stuff around becomes burdensome. It's tough enough dragging your own body around floor after floor of exhibit area without adding pounds of dead weight. And soon the gleaming relief of a trash can comes into view, and he unloads the whole pile without even a backward glance. Take a look at the wastebaskets at trade shows sometime if you really want to get depressed. They are packed with thousands of dollars' worth of literature.

How to avoid this gross waste? Don't distribute catalogs at a show!

The best technique is to answer the "Do you have a catalog?" gambit with "Surely. We'll be happy to send one to you. May we have your name and address?"

Keep a batch of catalog request cards on hand. The advantage of this method is threefold. First, you know the catalog will reach the buying prospect when he has time to read it and where he has the facilities accessible for sending in orders.

Second, this filling-in-the-card method gives you the golden opportunity to hold the guy in the booth while you are writing. And this forces him to look around. If you write slowly enough, he might have the chance to see everything you have. And maybe even become interested enough to buy something on the spot.

And third, you accumulate a list of likely prospects. You do need some literature at a show—throwaway material such as catalog sheets, circulars, or envelope stuffers. Why offer it at all if it will be discarded instantly? Because this material performs the same service as point-of-purchase displays in a store. It supplies the prospect with a product's salient selling features and all the important information that the existent salespeople do not know or the non-existent salespeople can't give.

Often, when the booth becomes crowded, a customer or browser will pick up a piece of literature and read while awaiting his turn. He can sell himself or pick up facts the booth salespeople may not remember to convey.

Just remember to keep all the literature accessible and neat. Nothing makes a booth look worse than assorted advertising literature littering the counters and floor.

GIVEAWAYS

The most repellent breed of show visitors are the booth-beggars.

"Whaddya giving away?" is the usual greeting of this charming bunch. A good kick in their bulging shopping bags is what they deserve—and all you should give them. Anyone who comes into the booth with that gimme attitude is not a serious buying prospect and should be ignored.

I am against show-time giveaways: I cannot see where they achieve any benefit for the donor, except to attract a lot of deadbeats who are looking for freebies, antagonize them when they are refused, and waste booth personnel effort in distribution. All in all, a big waste of money.

What's the point of giving gifts to someone who has already found your booth? The aim of every show promotion should be to draw traffic—but selected traffic. A booth that is jammed with the gimme gang looks busy, all right, and may cause much envious teeth-gnashing in your competitors' corners, but it produces zero business for you. In fact, prospective purchasers are often deterred by the crowd, so that nonbuyers could crowd out the buyers.

HOW TO PULL SELECTED TRAFFIC

There is a sure method of getting almost everyone on your mailing list to stop by your booth. It's a simple idea —so simple you wonder that it works so well. But it does—fantastically.

All you do is send out a mailing, no later than a month before the show, containing a gift certificate, "redeemable only in person at our booth." Now here's the secret ingredient. The gift *must* be something for a wife or daughter or granddaughter—a piece of jewelry suitable for a girl or woman.

The response will amaze you.

I remember the first time that I used this gift certificate approach, the sales manager predicted that the whole idea would be a surefire fiasco.

"You think any guy will bother to come in for a twenty-five-cent piece of jewelry?"

You should have seen his face as the steady trek of coupon-bearing buyers began streaming into the booth! He saw buyers who had just been faceless names on our mailing list for years, people who had never before visited our exhibit.

They bothered to come, all right. And the psychology is very simple. A man who has been away at a trade show usually returns home with a bit of guilt tucked into his bosom. Maybe he has a valid reason for the guilt, or maybe he's a nice guy who has had fun and feels sorry for the little woman who's been stuck home with the sick kids. So he likes to bring home little goodies. Especially a piece of jewelry that every girl is sure to love. It makes him feel like Santa Claus.

Then there's the coupon-signing-in-the-booth gambit. That's a plus for your side. Because he must stand there and sign his coupon before redeeming it. And the salesman must rummage around a bit to find the jewelry gift. And that all takes time—calculatedly so—time to allow the buyer to look around, maybe to pick up and idly inspect a product, which is an opening for a smart salesman to say: "That's our best-selling product. And believe it or not, you picked out the best-selling color!"

Now, some advice about the gift. It should be a classic-looking piece that appeals to all ages. And since it must be inexpensive to make mass distribution economically feasible, observe the rule that should be followed whenever buying any budget-price merchandise: Keep it simple. The less detailing on the piece, the less chance to expose sleazy workmanship.

The most successfully accepted piece I ever used was a pearl-drop pendant on a gold chain. Maybe because of the impressive legend on the box, "genuine cultured pearl, 14 kt. gold-filled chain," and then again, because of the classic simplicity of the jewelry. A gold heart on a chain is also a popular choice.

And it *must* be nicely boxed. Packaging is very important to convey genuine value. It usually comes in a small cotton-padded gold or white box, which looks very impressive. You can buy this sort of stuff from manufacturers of costume jewelry or from premium houses. Sometimes you can get a special closeout at a very good price. As for the price, I have never paid more than thirty-five cents apiece for this merchandise, boxed and all. Don't be afraid to haggle—you are buying a goodly quantity and should insist on a good price.

SHOW-TIME HINTS

The next thing you want to do after luring a live prospect into the booth is to crack open that order book. And that's sometimes harder than the pulling-in procedure.

It's a kind of a game you play. The customer pretends that he really just came by to look, and you pretend you just want to show him what's new. No one likes to mention that dirty word "order." Not right away, that is.

So how do you manage to make the transition from the

role of genial host to the one of crassly commercial order-taker? Gently.

That's where a prepared deal comes in—particularly a low-ticket one that includes something new. Here's how the dialogue goes:

CUSTOMER: Well, what have you got that's new?

SALESMAN: Here's our new number six-oh-seven, a completely new departure, something your customers will flip over.

CUSTOMER: Hmm—nice. How much?

SALESMAN: Only two twenty-five retail. Matter of fact, we're introducing it in this show-special deal—an assorted dozen for only twenty-five dollars. But you can only get this if you order it right here. Would you like one?

CUSTOMER: Well, okay, might as well.

Once the order book is open, it is up to the salesman to keep writing.

Besides the lower-ticket order opener deal, you should have many other preset "show-special deals" for all of your products. It makes it easier and faster for the salesman to sell, and once he gets the customer going in a buying mood, it's go-for-broke time.

Most show managements grandiosely offer participating exhibitors an unlimited supply of show invitations—imprinted with their specific booth number, yet. They suggest that you send them to your customers to tell them to come in and visit.

Now, why pay the postage of the weight of these cards when you can say the same thing right on your own mailing? You can print in a prominent spot, "See us at the

Now, why pay the postage of the weight of these cards when you can say the same thing right on your own mailing? You can print in a prominent spot, "See us at the X Show, Booth #002." And you've said it all. There is nothing gracious or individual about their invitation cards. You must realize that they are offered to all exhibitors, and chances are that your customer list is receiving the same card from other suppliers. The show management loves it; this is great advertising for them. But what's in it for you?

Second to "Where's the rest room?" the most-asked question at a show is "What's new?"

And it's natural. Most exhibitors use shows to introduce their new offerings, and most visitors come to find out about the latest innovations in the industry. So make it easy, and make it obvious. They have come to see it, and you have come to sell it.

Put whatever you have that is new—whether it's brand-new or you have added a widget and it's newly improved —*put it front and center* with a big, bold designation "NEW."

Ever see what a booth looks like after a siege of sales? Each product is strewn where the last man who handled it dropped it, and the place is a shambles. Unless you get the chance to tidy up again before the next wave of customers hits, everyone will be working under the handicap of being unable to find whatever it is they are trying to sell. And nothing loses a prospective purchaser's interest faster than waiting for a salesman to burrow through a pile of merchandise to find whatever it is he thinks the customer should buy.

The only way to prevent constant chaos is to have a collection of marked samples mounted permanently to the display. Additional stock can be loosely distributed around the booth. But the salesmen can always depend on finding a representative sample of every item whenever he needs it.

SETTING-UP TIME

There's nothing more dispiriting than standing amid a pile of unopened cartons in an un-set-up booth, knowing that you have to set it up. There's that helpless feeling of wondering how to begin and where to put what.

If you have some artistic ability or taste and experience, you will probably end up with an attractive-looking arrangement after a few sweat-soaked hours. But if, like most people, you have no ability in these directions, the end result is apt to look pretty grim.

That's why it is a good idea to have someone back in the home office, who has some talent, taste, and time, draw up a diagram—a simple drawing instructing the setting-up personnel just where each piece should go. This simple how-to-set-up-the-booth diagram will save hours of work and aggravation and insure a tasteful, attractive display.

HOSPITALITY SUITES

There is a feeling in some corners of industry that a free flow of liquor brings a big flow of business. I don't know on what instinct they base that opinion, because the facts surely don't back it up.

At every trade show there are always some "hospitality suites" around. A "hospitality suite," in case you are not familiar with the name, is a couple of hotel rooms taken over by a company, to which buyers are invited to pass the time of day and hoist a few in the name of friendship.

The aim of these alcoholic amenities is to influence the customers to be kindly disposed toward the host organization when buying time rolls around.

tion and canniness, any buyer could let his buying judgment be affected by free booze? Perhaps if all things were equal among a group of products, this show of hospitality could tip the scales. But all things are never equal, and the buyer must buy the best buy.

Perhaps the aim of the hospitality suite is to get the buyer into a noncommercial atmosphere and sell him softly in a social ambience. Maybe this works in a large company who has a rotating group of personnel to man the suite.

But a small company has a small executive roster. And the same crew has to be on duty pretty much of the time. Thus by about two o'clock in the afternoon the hosts are suffering from a severe case of overhospitality and not really sure what they're selling or to whom. And the image conveyed to buyers is apt to be of a company run by giggling, glassy-eyed executives with upside-down badges. It is not one to inspire confidence.

And then you run the risk of becoming a second home to the deadbeat boozers who inhabit every industry. If they are customers, you can't throw them out, so you're stuck.

All in all, for my money and yours, a hospitality suite is bad news.

CHAPTER 9

SALES MEETINGS

Sometimes when you're facing the sea of sullen sales faces, you wonder what masochistic madness prompted you to call this meeting in the first place.

It's a good question. Because if you've ever had the misfortune to be at a hotel when it was hosting a corporate sales meeting, and you see the sophomoric sybaritic bedlam that passes for pleasure among so-called grown men, you wonder what the company expected to accomplish by the bash.

Actually, the sales meeting has a very vital function in a company's sales-building structure. But today too many large corporations use sales meetings as payola for underpaid salesmen, and the valid basis for the meeting gets buried under a lavish mishmash of wine, women, wives, minks, and booze.

Fortunately, since we of the small business world don't have all that cash to cast about, sales meetings must be sales meetings. And they can be very effective.

LOVE AND CATHARSIS FOR SALESMEN

Salesmen want money, but they also need love. They spend their days currying the favor of bitchy buyers, courting rejection at every turn, trying to be not just liked, but well liked.

They need the ego satisfaction of corporate recognition. They need to know how important they are to the existence and future of the company.

That is one of the prime purposes of a sales meeting. To publicly acknowledge the salesmen's importance. It gives them a shot in the arm, a feeling of affinity to the company. They like to know that while they are out there doing battle among the hostiles, someone up there likes them and truly cares to know what they think, feel, and want.

A meeting is a great catharsis for them and allows them to air all their grievances. That's one of the things you have to watch for, though. Sometimes you get a couple of master gripers together, and the whole meeting can disintegrate into a tirade of complaints and self-pity.

Getting all the salespeople together can be very informative for them as well as for management. They get the important opportunity to exchange ideas, discuss mutual problems, and pass along solutions to one another. Chances are that a knotty situation the salesman in Duluth has now is much the same as the fellow from Akron handled last month. Each can learn from the other's success or failure.

If you hold the meeting in the company's hometown, you are able to take the sales force through the factory to familiarize them with new manufacturing techniques and often old production problems. A salesman tends to think in a very insular fashion. His concern is only his customer and his commission. But when they see the plant situation, they often get a new overview that helps them to understand why orders cannot always be shipped when and how they want them.

To customers the salesman *is* the company. His or hers is the face you present to the market. And you want that face to be a happy one; you want it to reflect a secure, solid situation.

The salesman should be 100 percent behind the company and not move over into the customer's corner when some difficulty arises. Sales meetings promote the salesman's feeling of belonging, of being a part of the organization, and help him to identify fully with the company.

PLANNING THE SALES MEETING

If you were laden with a lavish treasury of tax-deductible sales-promotional dollars, you could toy with a choice of exotic sites for meetings—from chartered ships to romantic islands. But since we are working close to the bone, there are only two economical methods of getting the sales force together. You can fly them all in to the company's hometown for a few days (or overnight), or you can wait for the annual trade convention.

Flying them to the company's hometown is the best way, because you have their undivided attention, and you have the various company facilities and personnel available within hailing distance.

However, this can be relatively costly, because you have their air fares and living expenses—and this can get to be a hefty tab. But if the budget can bear this, it can be an invaluable experience and an extremely worthwhile investment that will pay dividends all year.

The alternate method—waiting for the annual trade convention—is the economy version. Since all salesmen must attend their industry's annual trade convention, this is one way to get them all together, without having to spring for additional fares.

If they are manufacturer's representatives, they pay their own way to the convention. So you are spared even that. And if they are your own men, you would have had to pay for their trips to the convention city anyway.

How to Pick the Place

Your first step is to reserve a meeting room at a hotel, convention hall, or anywhere that is nearby and convenient.

Be fussy about the place. A sleazy, tacky room with rickety furniture and peeling paint does not convey a successful upward image to salesmen. Be alert to the ambience —it's important.

Look around at the decor; check into the service. Be sure it's a place that caters to meetings and has the proper facilities. Don't settle for a hotel dining room or suite that becomes an instant meeting room by throwing some green felt over a few tables.

Try to get a sunny, bright room. Cheerful surroundings can add immeasurably to the positive mood of a sales meeting.

And the size of the room is vital. Don't get a place that is so huge and cavernous that voices echo and intimacy is lost. Nor should it be so small that everyone is rubbing knees. Select the right size to accommodate your number of participants.

How to Pick the Time

Morning is preferred! Try to make it a breakfast meeting.

The morning is a far better time for many reasons. First, everyone is fresh and reasonably alert. Second, the early hour gives you a respectable reason to avoid the alcohol problem.

Booze has its place in living and business, but it has no place in a sales meeting. I know it's a stimulant and a lovely relaxant, but ever try to talk seriously to over-stimulated and overrelaxed salesmen? It can be a total waste of time and money. You can serve all the liquor you want after the meeting is over—but never before or during.

THE AGENDA

Before you start, be sure a pad and pencil have been placed before each salesman. At the onset of the meeting make a little announcement to the effect that they can use these pads to note down questions they would like to ask each speaker *after* the entire program is over.

No questions or discussion allowed during the program —and that's an order. I have seen interruptions and questions destroy speakers and even wreck an entire sales meeting. There was the time a company I was with had based their entire presentation around a new indestructible Mylar-laminated ring binder. That was when DuPont had just introduced Mylar, and it was hot news.

A sample of the Mylar-coated binder was placed in front of each salesman. (Mistake number one. A sample of each new product should be passed around as a speaker is discussing it—never left in front of the salesman throughout the meeting for him to play with.) The company sales manager made an enthusiastic speech about this exciting new book that was going to revolutionize binder sales and knock competition for a loop, because it was virtually untearable and uncrackable. While he talked, the company's number-one crank—a salesman who was known for his cantankerous bellicosity—was carefully picking away at the laminate, doing a thorough job of loosening the adhesion. By the time the sales manager was just hitting the pinnacle of his pitch, predicting a rosy economic future for all at the table if they just went out and pushed this superlative new product, Mr. Lovable raised his hand to ask a question: "You say this binder won't tear?" Whereupon he stood up and calmly ripped the cover right down the middle.

Utter bedlam ensued. No matter how we tried to explain that the binder would never tear with normal usage, that nothing is safe against misuse and vandalism, it was too late. The psychological damage had been done, and the whole presentation was shot. Six months of product development, advertising, and sales-promotion plans—gone.

If the salesman had been forced to save his question until the end of the entire meeting, after the production manager had explained the construction and qualities of the binder and after other subjects had been covered, the impact of this little bomb would have been lost. And of course, if he hadn't been given the chance to pick away at the product for an hour, the entire disaster would have been averted.

Some people are devout iconoclasts. They get a perverse pleasure out of tearing down what others build or believe in. These are the sort of adorable inquisitors that can break up a sales meeting with negative thinking and contentious questions. So head 'em off at the pass, and allow no questions or interruptions until all speakers have finished.

Speakers—How to Keep the Meeting Moving

The meeting of a small organization should always be opened with a short talk by the head of the company. This speech is usually intended to be in the inspirational vein, although most of them inspire nothing but boredom.

Since you, as the person concerned with communications and sales promotion, will probably write the speech, make it short and succinct. There's nothing that deadens a meeting faster than a long-winded, presidential-type rendition of clichés and homilies. Those recollections-of-past-glories lectures so beloved of company founders are guaranteed instant eye-glazers.

Avoid them. All a presidential opening speech should say is: "Glad to see you all here; we've had a great, exciting past, and let's look forward to a great, exciting, profitable future together. We can't miss when you hear all the great things our people have planned for the coming year, and let's get to it." Put it simply; maybe add a light touch here and there if you can. The sales force will always listen respectfully to the president of the company, but don't make it a punishment.

The sales manager is the person who makes the salesmen feel as if they have hitched their wagons to a star. The sales manager's pitch should be positive, exciting, action-packed, and filled with plans and promises.

What we did last year "you and us together." (Very important! Keep the "I's" out of all these speeches. It's "we" or nothing. After all, where would a sales manager be without salesmen to manage?) Then he unveils the plans for the coming year.

A good way to really get the salesmen in the palm of his hand is to personalize his talk. Include a one-by-one comment on each salesman's successful performance in the past. A mention of some specific large sale, some hard-to-crack account he finally won, some public statement of each man's achievement before his peers. The purpose of the sales meeting is to activate the salesmen. There's nothing like a little recognition to motivate a man to perform.

It is very important that the sales force be given a strong positive picture of the company and its future. I don't mean phony promises about riding off into the glowing sunset together. Nor any equivocation about any unpleasant facts and figures. Distortions court disaster.

If the past year has indeed been a poor one, face up to it, and explain the situation honestly. There's no sense trying to hide poor sales figures, because salesmen have an incredibly efficient grapevine. When something happens in the main office, they seem to hear of it almost as fast as the company switchboard operator (a breed whose intelligence-gathering system makes the C.I.A. look like the Boy Scouts). And official denials only add to the salesmen's apprehension.

As long as the ending note is a positive one—with a realistic assessment of the company's potential based on the vigorous new plans—the salespeople will be with you. Whatever last year has been, make them feel they are with a progressive, ambitious company and that any setback has been a temporary one. Keep them loyal, enthusiastic, and believing that they have a good solid future with the company.

The ad manager also delves into past history: a little review of last year's successes—"thanks to your cooperation," of course.

Now reveal the new advertising and sales-promotion plans for the coming year, and enlist their support, "which we need and depend on." Talk of the near future—and the distant future—of plans that are actually now in work and blue-sky brainstorms that will be coming along soon.

Now here's the man they have all been waiting for— the production manager. This is the "Mr. Unavailable" they can never get to see and talk to in the plant, because he's always harried and hassled with labor problems, delivery defections, slow shipments, production and machinery malfunctions.

But he's the man who knows how the products are produced and why they sometimes do not turn out exactly as the salesmen would like.

Write a short speech for him. *And allow him to deliver it sitting down.* Production managers are usually not too articulate and are often surprisingly panicked at the prospect of public speaking.

I say "surprisingly" because I remember my shock when I saw a production manager whom I was accustomed to hear howling at burly machine-operators, barking profanity-punctuated commands to teamsters, unable to stand before a sales meeting because his knees were trembling! And I remember being glad that I had written his speech on cards, because if it had been on paper, the rattle of the shaking sheets would surely have drowned out his words.

I have never been able to quite understand why speaking before a sales meeting terrorizes some people. I could understand it if the audience were composed of total strangers. But sales meetings are attended by people the speakers have talked to and worked with for years. There's rarely an alien in the house. Yet en masse they seem to present a threat that throws many an executive into a tizzy of tension. (The use of visual devices sometimes takes the speaker's mind off his fears.)

The production manager's talk should explain production problems so that the salesmen become more patient about delivery delays and more understanding about unfilled manufacturing demands.

Salesmen can be the most unreasonable of creatures. When customers ask for special adaptations or custom-made merchandise, the salesman naturally wants to take the orders. But these demands are not always realistic or feasible. And here's the time to explain why and equip the men with enough knowledge to know when to tell a customer that it cannot be done, rather than waste the time and effort of writing to the company.

Talk of new machines, if any, new production plans, and

new techniques that will expedite future production. Then close with a thanks for their patience and understanding.

The Question Period

Now the question-and-answer period. If you have done your work right, they'll be happy, and the questions will be good-humored. And they will be primed and refreshed, ready to go forth and multiply sales for another year.

THE SECRETS OF SMOOTH SPEECH-WRITING

Most executives say that they want to write their own speeches. It's a matter of pride, of course. But actually, they find it an onerous chore and tend to procrastinate. And when it finally does emerge, it is stiff, dull, and disorganized.

So how to write their speeches for them without impinging on their pride?

I have found a method that has worked well and avoids the dangers of damaged dignity and dull discourses.

A few months before the sales meeting, ask all participating executives to please "just jot down some notes" of what they want to cover—subjects they want to talk about in their speeches.

I stress the casual "just jot down" because the sound is less threatening and enables them to unbend and write easily. You can take their notes and "edit them," as you will diplomatically term the procedure, or in plain English, transform them into a speech.

To a nonwriter—that is, someone who does not write for a living—there is something apparently paralyzing about a blank piece of paper. (It's not always an easy thing for a professional writer to face, either.) Tell someone you want him to write a speech, and he will be totally unable to produce a word.

Somehow, people feel that words that go on paper must have a heraldic solemnity. And a "speech"! The very word conjures up images of majestic moving declarations at least as noble as Washington's farewell to his troops. So they ponder, suffer, and sweat. And painfully construct formal, "meaningful" sentences incorporating obscure polysyllabic words they haven't used since freshman English. And ultimately produce a peroration that has the spirit and verve of a last will and testament.

The best way to insure that your salesmen do not fall asleep is for you to write the speeches.

The secret of writing a good speech is incredibly simple: *Make it conversational.* Speaking to fifty people is no different from speaking to two; all you do it talk louder.

Use everyday, casual language, replete with contractions and colloquialisms, and they'll listen. But start packing your talk with "show-off syntax"—big words and formal phrases—and a deadly hush soon settles over the audience not because they're spellbound, but because they're asleep.

Organize the speech in three parts: First, state what you intend to accomplish. Second, enumerate how you intend to accomplish it. Last, sum up with a reiteration of the accomplishment.

VISUAL AIDS—THE RELAXERS

In the theater they call it stage business. It consists of actions and visual devices to keep the audience's eyes from wavering while the performer goes through a particularly long soliloquy.

Have you ever noticed actors' constant preoccupation with cigarettes and liquor? A consistent TV-watcher would get the idea that fully one-quarter of American adult life is spent finding, lighting, and smoking cigarettes and one-quarter spent finding, mixing, pouring, and drinking cocktails. Actually, these theatrical preoccupations are merely bits of stage business, activities dictated by the director to keep the actors involved in interesting movements while they make some pretty dull conversation. In effect, these are visual aids to keep the audience's attention.

Which is exactly the function of visual aids in sales meetings. Unless your speaker has the visual assets of Elizabeth Taylor plus the vocal attributes of Richard Burton, the audience can get pretty tired of looking and listening. After ten minutes of staring at a stationary talking object, eye-glaze time sets in.

It's important that you devise ways to get the speaker to move and to perform some operations of visual interest to the audience. These actions also serve to relax the speaker. As you may know, if you have ever addressed a group, the hardest thing to work out is what to do with your hands. Which is why the cigarette-lighting business is so popular. (One of the oldest theatrical cigarette-lighting gambits to insure prolonged audience attention is to strike a match and just hold it while continuing to talk. After a second the audience's collective eye becomes riveted to that flame, waiting for it to burn down to the smoker's fingers. You can be certain to hold the audience in thrall until the second you blow out the flame, when you can almost hear the sigh of relief.)

Visual devices take the speaker's mind off his stage fright. He has chores to perform and becomes too busy to be nervous.

There are a number of simple, inexpensive visual-aid devices you can use.

Blackboard

The blackboard is the most-oft-used accompaniment to speeches because it's easily found and most familiar. However, it is also the least effective.

The technique has the speaker highlight his talk with notes, graphs, and/or diagrams which he writes on the board as he talks—schoolteacher style.

The trouble with the blackboard method is that very few people know how to write on a blackboard. You have to write large; you have to apply the chalk firmly; you have to write clearly and in a straight line. And if you think that's easy, take your mind back to grade-school days when your teacher asked you to come up to the board and work out a problem before the class.

Most people have a lousy enough handwriting on paper but on a blackboard, it's an illegible impossibility.

The other drawback is that it takes too long to write the phrases or figures, during which time the speaker usually has his back to the audience—not a posture recommended to keep attentiveness high.

Magnetic Boards and Easels

These are various types of boards, sometimes called felt boards, that have a magnetic or adhesive quality; you just slap signs on, and they stick.

These boards are available from art-supply and stationery stores. But if you can't find them locally, you can make one easily with Velcro strips.

Velcro strips consist of two pieces of mutually attractive fabric. You merely paste one piece on your board and the mutually attractive piece in back of your sign, and it adheres on touch. Velcro can be bought in most needlework stores and sewing departments.

The purpose of signboards is merely to punctuate your talk—to point up highlights and build a complete story.

For instance, the ad manager is talking about a planned program of local promotions (as described earlier). To add drama and color to the talk, he would draw attention to the specific areas of attack planned and show the cumulative effect of the total assault by means of signs on the visual board.

The first sign would title the total aim of the campaign: "The Campaign to Capture Cleveland," and as he made the statement, he would slap the sign on top of the board. Subsequent signs, which he would put up to accompany the verbalized point, might say:

"Local Newspaper Ads"
"Dealer Tie-in"
"Cooperative Dealer Advertising"
"Direct Mail"
"Store Window Displays"
"In-store Displays"
"TV, Radio"
"Publicity Tie-ins"

And as the board builds up, the tremendous strength of the impending sales-promotional assault becomes visually as well as aurally apparent. It builds to the inescapable conclusion, the sign that reads, "Result: We Capture Cleveland!"

Building Blocks

Giant-sized children's playing blocks, usually made of board, make marvelous visual-aid devices.

You just paste a sign on the front of each block (and a number on back so that the speaker gets the sequence right). Instead of putting signs on a board, he stacks the blocks up point by point.

It's a very colorful device and more interesting-looking than a board. And you could always use the closing sign-line: "And that's how we build a structure of solid sales" or some other building-oriented phrase.

You can use flash cards, like schoolteachers use to teach the multiplication tables. Or slides. Or movies. You can rent slide projectors and make your own slides with special pencils. There are any number of visual aids you can make out of readily accessible materials. Just look around you, and be creative and unafraid. It doesn't have to be elaborate.

Good visual-aid devices do not have to be slick or costly. The simplest easel board can be as effective as the most elaborate presentation. You can hand-print the signs yourself or use stencil lettering (like they use in shipping rooms). Or get a local sign-painter to do them. It matters not what they are, merely what they do.

CHAPTER 10

THE SECRET OF A SUCCESSFUL CATALOG

"Sales stink. We'd better tell those salesmen to get off the golf links and start pushing in the field."

Nervous management always looks for a fall guy for falling sales, and the inevitable initial scapegoat is the salesman. It does seem logical to blame the order-taker for not taking orders. But jumping to conclusions in business can be a dangerous and costly exercise. Being too quick to settle on the cause for slower sales prevents the thorough analysis of other factors which may be the real cause of the trouble.

One of the prime failures of small-company management is not backing up their sales forces with the proper tools. And the prime sales tool is the company catalog.

The catalog is the very heart of a company's total selling effort. It is, in effect, the salesman's bible; he lives or dies by it in the field.

Ideally, the catalog should function in a two-pronged effect to secure business: 1) as a selling tool for the salesmen and (2) as a buying guide for the customers. This may sound like fancy semantics, but it's not. It involves a specific approach to the presentation of the company's products. A poorly arranged, confusing catalog that is incorrectly oriented can virtually cripple salesmen and prevent them from working at peak efficiency.

HOW TO PLAN AND ORGANIZE THE CATALOG

Group products according to how they are used, not how they are made. Products that are made together should not necessarily be sold together. How, where, and by whom the merchandise or service is used are the only factors that determine catalog groupings.

You may have two products that are virtually identical, except one has a widget on top for home use and the other has the widget on bottom for industrial use. Now, most non-promotion-minded executives tend to say: "Why waste catalog space and repeat the specifications twice? It's really the same item—just show one picture, and mention that it comes in two variations."

Fine. They've saved space and lost sales for both products. Because the buyer who is looking for a home widget gets thrown by an industrial-looking item. And the buyer seeking an industrial widget says, "That's not for me— that's a home product." So by cutting catalog space costs, they have also cut the catalog's selling effectiveness.

You must think in terms of how the buyer thinks and buys, and address yourself solely to his needs. Because two products are made with similar manufacturing technique or because they happen to be fashioned of the same material or have any other production similarities is of absolutely no interest to the buyer. When he's looking for a specific item, he expects to find it under the specific use category.

For instance, suppose you are preparing a retail jeweler's catalog and wish to advertise some gold charms that could be used on a woman's bracelet or on a man's neck chain. The expeditious space-saving way would be to show the charms and state, "For Men and Women." Sure, why not? It's the same item, isn't it?

But the real question is, Would a male buyer be likely to find it in the ladies' charm-bracelet section of the catalog? If he's looking for a medallion to suspend from his chain, he wants just that, and not an "also." The right, bright place to feature it is in the men's jewelry section, among the cuff links and signet rings. In other words, show the same piece twice, or three times, categorized according to its uses and users.

A clever merchandiser like Bergdorf Goodman, of Fifth Avenue in New York, demonstrated this specialized user approach by running ads that featured "Men's Gold Medallions" in a series before Christmas. These were actually the same medallions that were being sold as charms in the women's jewelry department. Result: doubled sales for the same item by capitalizing on its doubled use.

If you were preparing a catalog for a toys and hobby-goods wholesaler, and you had a butterfly net that is also used as a fish-tank scooping net, would you show it in the fish-tank equipment section or in the butterfly-catching equipment section? The answer, of course, is to show it in both sections with a completely different sales pitch each time. Because the fellow looking for a fish-tank net is going to hit the fish-tank section only, and the butterfly-catcher is not going to go flipping through the entire catalog to figure out where you might have elected to put his net.

Buyers are the busiest of people—and the least patient. They are not going to take the time to figure out puzzles or listen to salesmen's lengthy explanations. If they don't see what they are looking for fast, they'll pick up someone else's catalog. So categorize products according to appeal, not appearance. Place each item where the buyer expects to find it—not where it is convenient or economical for you.

Group products according to how they are bought. This calls for putting yourself in someone else's head. You have to figure out how a buyer thinks when he is planning a purchase of your particular type of product. Does the customer buy in terms of style, price, size—or what? Every field is different, and the best way to find out the buying idiosyncrasies of your industry is to tackle those walking treasure troves of market information—the company salesmen.

Talk to the salesmen, chat with the order clerks—anyone involved with taking orders. Find out just how customers *ask* for your products. And arrange your catalog groupings accordingly. For instance, suppose you're offering some sort of monthly service, such as office maintenance or bookkeeping or public relations. You may learn that the question most commonly asked by potential clients is, "What can I get for about two hundred dollars per month?" Or perhaps you are cataloging eyeglass frames. The salesmen might mention that most customers want to know which frames they can get for under twenty dollars or ten dollars. Or maybe you are with a food importer whose customers frequently ask for gourmet foods that retail for under two dollars. If price turns out to be the major purchasing factor in your field, then the wisest thing would be to group your products or services according to cost. For instance, a page devoted to twenty-dollar spectacles, another page showing ten-dollar glasses, and so on.

In the ring-binder field buyers think in terms of soft cover or hard cover, three-rings or multo-ring. So if you were preparing a ring-binder catalog, you would group products according to these elements. Now, that may sound like simple logic. But when you realize that this means a single binder cover becomes four different products and should appear in four different places in the catalog, you may have some idea of the problems ahead.

For as I've mentioned, working in small or medium-sized businesses means you are usually working closely with production managers and other non-promotion-minded management. All they know is that this is the same binder cover, with some minor variations.

You have the task of explaining that each variation transforms it into an entirely different product: a soft-cover three-ring, a hard-cover three-ring, a soft-cover multo-ring, a hard-cover multo-ring. You can see where you may have some difficulty in conveying your concept. But don't let them deter you. They may know how to make it, but you know how to market it.

In the lamp trade people generally buy according to incandescent and fluoresecnt. There are many other selective factors, of course, but that's the basic one. And that would be your primary cataloging division. In a furniture catalog you would probably classify according to style periods—contemporary, provincial, and so on. In publishing you would undoubtedly arrange according to subjects.

HOW TO USE SUGGESTIVE SELLING

Remember the days when if you asked the druggist for a toothbrush, he suggested toothpaste? And when you bought shoes, the dealer asked if you needed polish or shoe trees? And if you bought shelving paper, the dealer asked if you needed thumbtacks?

That's called suggestive selling, and it's still one of the most effective ways of upping a sale. You can apply this technique when you are preparing a catalog by showing interrelated products together. If there are accessories involved with a product, show them on the same page.

If it's a toy catalog, list batteries next to all battery-operated toys. If it's a calendar catalog, list next year's pads with the base. If it's a cosmetic catalog, list refills right along with the pressed powder compact, eye-liner, and so on.

This is the simple procedure of reminding the buyer of related items that he might need in conjunction with the purchase he has just made. He's happier that you performed the service of advising him what he will need to have the item he's just bought work properly. And you're happier because you have achieved the greatest possible buying potential from the catalog.

Of course, this does not preclude the necessity of featuring these same accessories in their own combined category. Thinking in buyer's terms again, remember there are many times that a purchaser merely needs refills or accessories (sometimes even for someone else's products, but why be proud—a sale's a sale). He should not have to figure out where you have placed them. A page or section headed "Accessories" will take him right to it.

MIX AND MATCH PRODUCTS

Okay, you've found the right way to group your particular items, and it works. What's to stop you from also having a few pages of alternate groupings to pull more sales mileage out of the catalog?

Say you have arranged products according to style. It might be a good idea to introduce a page of "under $50" items. This is especially effective in retail catalogs, much as department stores set up "Gifts under $10" and "Gifts under $5" tables around Christmas time. It facilitates selection by the many ambivalent customers who know what they want to spend but not what they want to buy.

Or if you have used price as your grouping basis, have a page or two of selected items that conform to one style or type. For lamps it could be "Student Lighting Suggestions." For furniture you might have "Young Homemaker Styles." Or you might just single out particular good buys from each section of the catalog and create a special category called "Especially Good Values."

DIVERSIFIED CATALOGS CAN CREATE NEW MARKETS

Most companies love to put out one big catalog consisting of everything they make. They're proud of their whole line and want to impress customers with the sheer volume of their output.

As a result, a prospective purchaser of, let's say, industrial building adhesives may have to wade through pages showing jeweler's cement, library glue, and other items of total disinterest to him. Chances are he won't even bother, but if he does, he's not impressed—he's distressed. The company has wasted the costs of cataloging and mailing unnecessary pages and has possibly destroyed the sale by catalog overkill.

There is absolutely no purpose in lumping everything together under one cover merely because they are made under one roof. Each market should have its own catalog, with products described in terminology familiar to that market. Here's how the diversified-catalog technique can be used to create new markets.

We had a client who made commercial ring binders that were also sold as photo albums. They knew there was a large market for albums, yet their sales in the photo field were negligible. They asked us what we could suggest in the way of promotion to increase their album sales.

Since the catalog is usually the key to a company's approach to marketing, that's the first place we looked. And there was the answer. Each page showed a stark ring binder and carried the legend "Used for home and office, for sales presentations and photos."

Simple, neat, and from the manufacturer's point of view, what could be righter? But from the buyer's point of view, nothing could be wronger. For one thing, since the catalog was originally and principally aimed at the office-equipment field, specifications were oriented to the commercial buyer. Capacity was shown in terms of how much data and how many charts the binder could hold. Terms were used such as "ring mechanism" and "gauge acetate." Adjectives such as "tough, heavy duty."

Now, when people want a lovely, sentimental photo album, they don't want a durable ring binder. It's all in the words and adjectives—what attracts one buyer repels another. True, the company salesman would tell his retailer customers that these binders were really exactly the same as albums. But how would that help the retailer when *his* customer asked questions? The catalog must provide the retailer with the familiar terminology that enables him to present the selling points within his customers' frame of reference. If you handicap him with the necessity of translating, forget it—you've lost him and the sale.

All we did was to make a separate catalog for photo albums. The same commercial binders were shown, but did they look different! They were pictured in decorator settings, described from the use and viewpoint of a photo album (i.e., capacity in terms of how many snapshots it stored).

Suddenly the firm had a full line of photo albums. Their salesmen were now equipped with a specialized selling tool that enabled them to approach photo shops and talk in their language. Result: A new market was opened that became a very lucrative source of sales.

Sometimes you can get an idea for a new market potential in the wildest way. I was visiting a friend in the hospital once and happened to notice that the lamps over her bed and on the mobile examination table were made by one of our clients. When I later mentioned this fact to the client, he said: "Sure. We make special voltage and wiring adaptations of many of our regular lamps for hospitals."

Following up on that casual lead, we culled all the lamps, plugs, stands, and accessories that were applicable to the hospital and medical field and created a special "Hospital and Medical Lighting Catalog." This led to the establishment of an entirely new sales division and a new and extremely profitable market for the company.

A cookware manufacturer might put out a separate catalog for industrial cookware equipment. A food broker might put out a catalog of organic foods. A bank might put out a catalog of "savings and money-management plans for widows."

The possibilities are as unlimited as the applications of the products or services you are selling.

HOW TO ARRANGE THE CATALOG

All too often, the writer of a catalog is so enamored of the sturdy construction features of his product or the fine way in which it performs its function that he forgets to stress what the function *is*.

The prime rule in writing a catalog is that old cliché "First things first." There's no point in telling a guy how great your product is unless you first tell him what it's for!

When a buyer is flipping through a catalog, he is seeking specific information, and he wants the facts fast, without digging through tons of flowery verbiage. If dig he must, forget it. One of the most frequently committed catalog sins is the burial of vital product specifications in a solid paragraph of prose. A catalog is no place to go creative. There is a basic framework that must be followed—a consistency of style that the buyer can rely on. He wants certain facts about every product and wants to see them in the same place on each page. This gives an orderliness to the catalog that facilitates ordering procedures.

The introduction to the catalog is the institutional image-building "see how great we are" schmeer that should appear on the inside front cover. It is usually the part of the catalog read more carefully, and more agonized over by the head of the company. Remember, this puts into words all the pride he feels over his accomplishments and status.

Here is a good place to have a picture of the plant and/or offices; shots of employees at work; a map pinpointing international distribution. Whatever elements you can conjure up that will represent the position of the company in the industry.

If you really want to pour it on, you can have a heart-warming "message from the president." You'd be surprised at how many people read it, besides the president and his mother.

The basic facts about ordering, terms and buying conditions, should be shown immediately, usually on page two or three, often next to the table of contents. F.O.B. where, company policy about returns, shipments, and so on.

HOW TO ANALYZE PRODUCTS
FOR BUYING FEATURES

Before setting up the individual pages, it is necessary to analyze the underlying features of each product. Again we turn to the poor man's market-research bureau—the company salesmen. Go over your current catalog with them, and find out what specifications customers want most to know about each product.

The basic questions most prospective purchasers want answered are:

1. What does the product do?
2. Where is it used, and by whom?
3. How does it do it better than competitive products?
4. How is it made?

These are the selling points that will convince him of the value of your products. Now he's ready for the specific selection process. Now he needs the buying features—construction factors he must know in order to get the version that most closely meets the need of his situation. This means colors, capacities, how it's packed, what it comes with, etc. If you want a simple guide as to what "buying feature" information should be included, just think of what facts your shipping or billing department needs for processing an order.

THE PAGE SETUP

What appears on top of each page to instantly identify each product should appear consistently in the same form, in the same spot, on every page. One of the most frequently used headings is the model number of the product followed by its name. It might read, "Model 756 The Windsor Series."

Now, why not just state the name, and leave the model number for the tables? Because usually no one knows the product name except the boss and his wife. In a small business the job of making up names for products is usually placed in the highly creative hands of the head bookkeeper or someone equally qualified. That's why you get such a redundancy of product names in many industries. How many times have you seen heavy-duty products named Hercules? Or a classic-styled classy product named Majestic? Or a service company called Acme?

The purpose of the page heading is instant identification, and the most commonly used appellation *among the buyers* (not the sellers) should be used.

Following the heading is the descriptive data. Here you might start with some prose, just a few lines generally extolling the lead features and uses of the product. Then come the details. Using the information gleaned from your analysis of buying features, evolve a basic format of captions that can be applied to every product, arranged in order of their importance. An example for a lamp catalog would be: where used; shade design; construction; finish; colors; comes equipped with; packed; bulb recommended.

The ultimate distillation of information is the ordering table and is usually the second thing looked for on each page. This table should be at the bottom of each page, with columns arranged in order of ordering details: (1) model or style number, (2) size, and (3) description.

It's easier for the buyer to have price right along with the product specifications. And in a retail catalog that's mandatory. But with the tremendous fluctuation of prices in raw materials many companies find they cannot afford to get locked into a list price for the life of a catalog. So if you are in an industry that has to accept price fluctuations as a fact of life, prepare a separate price list that can be changed often with economic feasibility.

One of the handiest devices, and most frequently used, in the entire catalog is the back-page index. It involves a tremendous job of collation but is well worth it. It is simply a listing of all the company's products in *numerical* or *alphabetical* order. Four columns that state: model number, price (if included), shipping weight (if an important buying consideration), and last, the page number on which the item appears in the catalog.

Now, this may seem like a nothing, but I have seen this index page face up on more desks than any other part of the catalog. Think of the convenience and ready reference it offers. Most customers, company employees, and sales clerks know the company products by style or model number. This index gives them an instant method for finding a specific product.

HOW TO DESIGN THE CATALOG

The cover is the grabber. After all, that's what stops them, that's what encourages and invites a buyer to open your catalog. That's why the design is vital.

If the design can integrate a representation of your products, fine. But that should not be the governing factor—not if it harms the design potential of the cover. Just be sure it is strong, has impact, and hits hard like a billboard.

Now the inside. Here you must think in terms of *spreads*, not single pages. Remember, the eye sees both pages simultaneously and should therefore be considered as one design entity.

Simplicity and *good photography* are the imperative factors. Too many design gimmicks can overpower the data you are presenting. Keep it clean, clear, and simple. And clear, factual photography is vital. This again is no place to get too arty—not if it obscures the product in any way. The prospective customer wants to see what he is buying in as sharp detail as possible.

Black-and-white catalogs can be quite smart. If that's what the budget dictates, contrasts can be achieved by reverses (white on black) or bendays (grays).

Color can be a most effective device in catalog layout and design. Not only does it break up the monotony, but it can be used to give a change of pace subjectively as well as aesthetically. For instance, you can single out important selling points in color. Or you can consistently put all refill information in color. Or you can distract from the sameness of two items by silhouetting one against a color and showing the other against white.

Here's an inexpensive trick that enables you to have a third color at no extra cost! A catalog is printed in "forms," which means a group of pages. There are three forms of eight pages each in a twenty-four-page catalog. Each form is run on the press separately. You can have the printer run each form in a different two-color combination; first one in black and red, second in black and green, third in black and yellow. He is actually printing only two colors at a time, so that's all you pay for. (He will charge you about twenty-five dollars for washing up the press after each run, that's all.) When the catalog is bound together, you will have an interspersing of colors that will make the book most exciting and impressive.

HOW TO MAIL THE CATALOG

The envelope should immediately identify the contents as a catalog. This prevents recipients from putting it aside and possibly burying it forever under a pile of third-class mail.

No one discards a catalog. It is of immediate interest to everyone it goes to. Buyers need them and look for them, because catalogs are the tools of their trade. Just state boldly on the outside of the envelope: "This is your NEW CATALOG 833."

Another way of achieving the instant identification effect is to use polyethylene pliofilm bags for mailing. A number of magazines are now mailed this way, with address labels affixed in the corner. The advantage is apparent (pun intended). The recipient sees what it is the minute the catalog hits his or her desk.

Many companies like to enclose a letter. If there is something to be said that cannot be included in the catalog,

Before: Note the lack of cohesion—the specifications and features scattered about so that the eye doesn't know where to settle. Also observe that pertinent accessories are shoved into various corners. And ... how about that line art that shows nothing of the true look of the product?

After: Notice how the important buying features are called out instantly. There is a convenient table at the bottom, and all the accessories are grouped together under the heading "MOUNTING VARIATIONS AVAILABLE." Also notice how the dimensions of the lamp are used as a design element in the upper corner of each spread instead of being buried in the copy somewhere. The product is shown photographically, with closeups and interesting "in use" arrangements.

165

such as price structure, new corporate policy, etc., this is the place to state it. But it had better be important to warrant the additional expense of inserting, plus printing.

Of course, you want to call attention to new products; buyers like to know of that at once. In fact, "What's new?" is usually the first question they ask when presented with a new catalog. You can call out the new products on a memo that may be clipped to the catalog or inserted in it. But again, this is a costly affair. And the "new" signal can be indicated with graphics on the catalog pages themselves.

Don't forget the order cards! Since you've spent a whole catalog presenting and selling your wares, it would be gross folly to overlook giving a method of buying them.

It's true that many buyers prefer to send in orders on their own purchase-order forms. But there's nothing handier and more conducive to buying than bound-in order cards.

The form is pretty simple—just a columnar arrangement for style number, quantity, etc. Here is the place to add that important line: "Please send me _____ additional copies of this catalog."

There are undoubtedly many other members of the customer company who have buying influence (for instance, their own salesmen). The more catalogs you have in effective buying hands, the more merchandise you will sell.

Avoiding Postal Perils

Here's a bit of advice that can save you heartaches, headaches, money, and maybe your job.

Before you go ahead with any printing or purchasing, have a dummy facsimile made of the entire catalog mailing. The printer will make up a bound dummy on the exact weight paper proposed. The envelope-maker will give you a sample of the exact weight envelope you plan to use.

Then insert a dummy memo, letter, order cards—whatever you intend to include in the catalog mailing—and take it to your local post office for their okay.

You may be shocked to find that two less pages will make a huge difference in postage cost. Or a slightly lighter weight paper. Or the inclusion of a letter may change the postal classification and throw you into a more costly category. And of course, they'll tell you the current regulations for specifications that must be printed on the envelope to insure the return of undeliverable catalogs. They are too costly to be lost forever in dead mail.

Try to get someone in the post office to sign his okay on your facsimile catalog mailing. However, that's pretty tough, since postmasters are past masters at eschewing responsibility and commitments.

Postal authorities can be quite sticky, arbitrary, and implacable. I've heard stories that would make strong men blanch. Like the company ad manager who learned, after the catalogs were all neatly sealed and stamped and delivered to the post office, that his last-minute addition of four pages moved the catalog into the next mailing class, which cost five cents more per envelope. When you're mailing thousands of catalogs, that runs into big cash.

HOW TO CUT DOWN CATALOG ERRORS AND COSTS

There is some perverse chord in human beings that causes them to relish the discovery of errors in printed material, especially catalogs. Mistakes are bound to occur in a compilation of data as extensive as a catalog. No matter how carefully you check and recheck, some point will be overlooked. And you, of course, will be held totally responsible.

To reduce that threat to a minimum, here's the fail-safe

procedure I have always followed. When you have completed the first copy draft of the entire catalog, Xerox it, and distribute copies to every conceivable individual in the company who can come down on your head later (and incidentally, whose opinions and advice may be very helpful). Write the person's name on his copy—that puts him on notice that opinions are being recorded for posterity, and if he overlooked something now, he can't holler about it later. Then attach a note asking for opinions, suggestions, etc., and demand a "must be returned by" date.

When you have your first set of proofs in hand, follow the same procedure. You may have to pay the printer for a few extra sets of proofs, but it's worth it. At this point those interoffice nit-pickers can be invaluable as proofreaders because they are looking only for errors, while you have been evaluating content.

After you have all copies returned and have integrated all valid corrections, then and only then, go ahead and print. And the day that the new catalog is distributed in the office, make up a brand-new big file folder ostentatiously labeled "Next Year's Catalog." Then when the first character comes in to gloatingly point out the error he found on page 21, you can just thank him coolly, and with great aplomb slip his notation into the folder and continue with your work.

CHAPTER 11

WRITING A SALES LETTER

It's Monday morning, and you're in the midst of trying to find your desk under the pile of morning mail and to adjust your weekend metabolism to the weekday tempo— and a salesman walks in.

"Good morning, valued customer," says he with a smile. "I want to thank you for your favors past, present, and future."

What would you do? Probably after checking the outer office to see if his keeper is waiting, you'd chuck the nut out.

Now, if that's how you would handle a man talking like that, think how fast you would dump a letter that rambled along in that archaic jargon.

Yet, for some unfathomable reason, businessmen persist in loading their letters with stilted, antiquated language that conjures up images of clerks in celluloid cuffs.

There seems to be some misconception in the halls of commerce that phrases like "We humbly beg your indulgence" or "We are deeply grateful for your past business" give the business letter a dignified, impressive tone.

169

Maybe it did fifty years ago, but today that kind of talk is anachronistic and totally ludicrous. Especially when these expressions of craven humility come from some crude commercial cutthroat who couldn't care less if you dropped dead—as long as it wasn't in the middle of the season.

The language in any letter should be succinct, simple, and to the point. You have something to say—that's why you wrote the letter in the first place. Then say it straight out, and don't entangle your statements in a mass of rhetorical sludge.

THE SUREFIRE FOUR-STEP SYSTEM FOR SUCCESSFUL SALES LETTERS

Like most things, it's not hard to write a successful sales letter once you know what to do and what not to do. I've just told you what not to do; now let's get to the "how to's."

During my years of writing sales letters and teaching others how to write them, I have evolved a system of rules —an outline to follow when composing and creating sales correspondence. I guarantee that if you follow this procedure, you will turn out the best, most effective sales letters you have ever produced.

Step 1. The pull-in (Grab attention instantly.)

Step 2. Make your point. (Announce your offering and extol its benefits.)

Step 3. Tell him what he must do to get it. (Where, how, how much.)

Step 4. Impel him to do it right now.

Now let's take it step by step.

Step 1: The Pull-In

Every letter must begin with an attention-grabber—the means of beguiling the reader to read on. We can divide these devices into two categories: gadgets that cost and gimmicks that don't. Naturally, since this book is designed for the economy-minded entrepreneur, we'll begin with the second category—gimmicks that are free and easy.

It's amazing how many simple things you can do to a letter to make it distinctive. Remember that distinctive merely means different; anything that can be readily differentiated from its peers is automatically distinctive. Among the guests at a Park Avenue dinner party the man of distinction would be the slob in an undershirt. And if sloppiness caused instant standout, we can use it to advantage in sales letters.

FINGERPRINTS AND SMUDGES

Most mail arrives in pristine condition, carefully typed and neatly spaced. Think of your double take if you opened an envelope and drew out a letter that was decorated with a few large smudges and finger marks. (Notice I said "a few." Don't get carried away and turn the pages into an unappetizing, unreadable mess.) There are a number of transitional lead-ins you could then use. For example, if you were promoting a hairdresser or a clothing store: "Your fingerprints are unique, distinctively, personally you. Just as your hairstyle [or clothes] should be individually, personally you."

If you are advertising a repair or maintenance service of any kind: "Does it pay to dirty your hands on repairs that you are really not equipped to handle? Why not let a professional do the job."

If you were promoting protective plastic envelopes: "Grime doesn't pay. If that thumbprint obscured a critical digit in a job specification, you could have a thousand-dollar error. Protect your job tickets in plastic envelopes."

CUTOFF CORNER

Here is a very simple trick that makes any letter instantly different. Just have the printer slice a diagonal chunk from the top corner of the sheet. Think of the many ways you can use this device to lead into a telling point. Try this for openers: "There are many ways for manufacturers to cut corners, but this is the *only* way you will ever see *us* do it."

Think of the many ways you can use this opening to unleash a blast at price-cutting, corner-cutting competition that you've been dying to tell off for years.

Or: "Trying to cut corners to make ends meet? Why not let us help out with a loan to tide you over until . . . ."

HANDWRITTEN LETTER

Who says a sales letter must be typewritten? Among the usual run of neatly typed letters the casual quality of a handwritten message is a sure stopper. Print it in blue ink on yellow blue-lined legal-pad paper, and you convey an intimacy that will be extremely effective.

Of course, the tone of such a letter must be informal. None of that "Gentlemen: In response to yours of the 5th," etc. This sort of medium lends itself to a light-banter-style message, the sort of thing that might conceivably be construed as a first-draft hastily-jotted-down interoffice memo. That doesn't mean it must be you who does the jotting. If your handwriting, like mine, resembles the berserk machinations of an ink-covered centipede, shop around for local talent. Check the office for some nice mature person who went to school in the days when the Palmer method meant penmanship and not golf.

UNDERSCORES, CALL-OUTS, ARROWS

Circle an important point, underscore it, or just draw a freehand arrow. Or make some marginal handwritten notation like "Don't forget this!" Have the printer reproduce these call-outs in blue or red, so that they look like they've been actually inked in. These break up the monotonous look of a letter, giving it a rough and readable quality.

IRREGULAR SPACING

A mass of aligned words looks tidy but dull. Avoid an appearance of total sameness. There are no points awarded for neatness or consistency, so juggle things around a bit. Indent a few lines that make a particularly telling point. Make one paragraph narrower and line it up all flush left. Make another one narrow, all flush right. The important thing is to keep the eye moving, to make the page varied and aesthetically interesting.

SKIP THE SALUTATION

"Dear Sir" or "Gentlemen" or "Dear Customer" hardly add a personal touch to the letter. So why bother? A letter can be a letter without a salutation. If it appears on letterhead paper, with a signature beneath, that conveys a letter. Try starting your letter with a catchy headline.

THE PERSONAL STORY

Comedians make their living mocking themselves; why not letter-writers? Begin a letter with some personal difficulty that you beseech the reader to help you solve. For instance, it's always open season on henpecked husbands, shrewish wives, nagging in-laws, and so on. It gets you instant interest and amused sympathy.

I once used this device successfully in a letter that was sent out just before the company catalog. The purpose of the letter was to pave the way for the soon-to-be-mailed catalog, to prime the customer for its imminent arrival. The success of the letter, and the fact that it was read, was proved by the tremendous number of personally directed comments that began to show up on orders.

Rye, N.Y. 10580

Please—save my homelife by reading the new V.P.D. catalog that you will receive soon.

My wife, Cynthia Smith, has been slaving away over this new catalog for the past six months. She's worked like a dog, and I've lived like one. Nothing but frozen foods for dinner and cold silence for company while she devoted herself completely to describing the glories of the tremendous range of new and old products.

Now after all that effort—can you imagine what it will be like to live with her if the catalog is not a success?

So please, for pity's sake—READ IT CAREFULLY.

It will be for your sake, too, because you'll find the new catalog will be a most valuable buying and selling tool. It will be a pleasure to use because:

1. It's step-indexed enabling you to turn to the product category you seek in seconds.
2. It's the only catalog of its kind to contain everything you need in plastic products and presentation binders.

As you can see, I've caught some of Cynthia's tremendous enthusiasm for V.P.D. products. But that's nothing to what I'll catch from her if her catalog is anything less than a tremendous success.

So I beg you—when you get the new Joshua Meier V.P.D. catalog within the next few weeks, please READ IT CAREFULLY AND BUY. Cynthia will be watching the mail anxiously. The smooth flow of my homelife will be determined by the flow of your orders. PLEASE—READ AND THEN WRITE . . . RIGHT AWAY!

> With heartfelt thanks,
> Sincerely yours,
> DAVID SMITH (Cynthia's husband)

These are just *some* of the gimmicks that take little more than ingenuity. Now to the gadgets that you can *buy* to liven up your sales correspondence.

Suppose you received a letter than began: "Keep your eyes on Hawthorn Books, Inc., where big things will be happening." And right there, pasted on top of the letter, were two little plastic eyes that actually moved.

Or a letter that had a miniature telephone pasted next to the words "Announcing a new Direct Hot Line to our plant."

You'd be intrigued, wouldn't you? So much so, in fact, that you most probably would read through the entire letters. And maybe even hold on to them for a while because you sort of hated to throw out those cute little gadgets.

There is a whole catalog-full of these three-dimensional miniatures with flat backs, ready for pasting on letters, to excite instant interest in sales correspondence. From tiny shovels and shotguns to buckets and bowling balls—there are hundreds of these devices that lend themselves to clever tie-in phrases that would make great opening gambits for sales letters. The company that offers this bonanza-packed catalog is Hewig Marvic Company, 861 Manhattan Avenue, Brooklyn, New York 11222.

I don't like to tout any company (especially one I have no stock in), but this firm is an absolute boon to sales-letter writers and to all small-business promotion people. It offers a tremendous range of gimmicks, gadgets, and motivational merchandise in any quantity from 25 to 25,000. It means that if you have just 100 letters to send to special customers, you can afford to make them exciting and effective. They offer things like invisible-ink letters (dip them in water, and the message appears), stock four-color illustrated letterheads that you can print a one-color message on, and a host of other products that can spark creative direct mail. Get on their mailing list—it's free—and you'll be fed a steady stream of attention-getting ideas.

Step 2: Make Your Point

I have a standard technique for instant improvement of almost every sales letter. Just cut off the opening paragraph, and bring the closing one up to the top. Try it. Nine out of ten times, you'll have a better, more forceful letter. Many people subscribe to a squeamishness about coming right to the point, like it just ain't nice to blurt out one's business until a suitable period of chit-chat has been observed.

In Eastern countries it is considered the height of business boorishness to plunge into crass commercial discussion immediately. One must pursue a ritual of deference and delicacy, and the topics of trade may never be touched upon until after the second cup of tea. It's a lovely and gentle way of working that never quite took hold here. Somehow, I can't quite visualize a salesman delicately balancing a porcelain cup as he discusses the history of civilization and the state of his wife's health with a smiling, courtly purchasing agent. A paper cup of lukewarm instant coffee while they haggle over price, maybe.

Hereabouts, you get down to basics fast, on a call or in a letter. If you put off the point, you put off the reader. Patience is not part of our commercial culture, and delay means death. You must convey the main idea of your letter immediately, or the busy reader may never wait around to find out what it's all about.

After the hopefully provocative lead paragraph, describe your offering. Simply, factually. What it is, how the reader will benefit.

Step 3: Tell Him What He Must Do to Get It

How much does it cost? What does he have to do to get it? This is the nuts-and-bolts information the reader needs in order to buy. If there's an order card enclosed, tell him.

Step 4: Impel Him to Do It Right Now

This is the crucial point—the activator. If your letter has been successful, the prospect wants to order by the time he reaches the end of the letter. Now we're in the danger zone. Will he buy now, or will he put the letter aside to attend to later? If he puts it down, you're through. Later means maybe, and maybe usually means never. The letter gets buried beneath the next day's mail and the next day's, and soon it becomes part of a messy pile that gets thrown out in bulk.

You must create the push to act immediately. "Order now, because this is a LIMITED OFFER good only until . . . ." This is the standard technique, and it works surprisingly well. Give a cut-off date or some imposed limitation that will mean they risk missing out on this great opportunity unless they *act now.*

Another strong simple way is just to say it straight: "Delay, and you may miss out on this tremendous, once-a-year opportunity. Don't put this letter down until you have sent in your order!"

All you must remember when you close a letter is, if you want the order, it's *now* or never!

Here is an actual sales letter given to me for some "improvement" by a sales manager. It is a perfect illustration of the kind of garbled material ground out every day by small-company executives who are totally uninstructed in sales-letter writing. It's a classic case of what not to do and why everyone who is responsible for creating commercial correspondence should get some training (or at least read this book!).

TO A VALUED CUSTOMER!

We are enclosing our new 1972 Kleer-Vu Price List which covers our entire packaged line of report covers, page protectors, pencil cases, photo accessories, and our award-winning wallet inserts.

Your profit on this Kleer-Vu line represents one of the highest levels in the industry, and we want to play a game with you in the hope that you'll expand the number of our items you are carrying.

The game which we call our "Lucky Seven-Eleven Promotion" will bring you only prizes and profit. It costs nothing to play, and it's very easy to be a winner.

Write an order for seven out of the fifty-nine items that are on the price list for a total of $700, and we will send directly to you or anyone you designate an AM/FM Digital Clock Radio in a radical new, cube design. This item has a retail value of $59.95.

If you can use more than seven items, write an order for eleven items totaling $1,100, and we will send you, or anyone you designate, a beautiful AM/FM Stereo with eight-track tape receiver built in. This will come complete with matching two-way horn speakers.

Kleer-Vu wants you to have these items both as a thank you for past business and as an incentive to add more of our very profitable items to your line.

The rules of the game are simple: (1) Call your Kleer-Vu representative right now or write the order and send it directly to this office. (2) Be sure your order covers seven items and totals $700 if you want the digital clock radio. (3) Make sure that your order totals eleven items and is for a total of $1,100 if you want the AM/FM Stereo cartridge. (4) Be sure your order calls for delivery prior to April 15.

Fill out clearly on your order, or on the attached form, the gift you want and the name and address of the person you want it sent to.

Both of these prizes are great for your office or your home— the Kleer-Vu line is great for your profit and has been known for years and years for the best customer acceptance in the industry.

We've got a quality product and we count on you—our distributor—to sell it. This is our way of thanking you for favors past, present, and future, and we certainly hope you'll play "Lucky Seven-Eleven" game with us.

Our best regards, and we hope you have a banner year.

Sincerely yours,

Now let's tear it apart.

1. Note the hot salutation and sparkling opening paragraph.

2. Note how much monotonous verbiage has to be penetrated before you reach the point of the letter—that this is a promotion that offers valuable free gifts.

3. Note the phony ring of the sixth paragraph: We want you to have these items to thank you for past business. Nobody buys that sanctimonious stuff. It introduces a hypocritical touch that threatens the credibility of the entire letter.

4. Note the waste of the good hook: "Be sure your order calls for delivery prior to April 15." A weak throwaway of the order-impelling fact that this is a limited offer.

5. Note the schmaltzy do-nothing closing, which maybe doesn't matter, since I strongly doubt that many people would ever read down far enough to see it.

6. Note how many words were used to cover what could be said in half the space.

7. Note the use of the celluloid-cuffs school of language: "To a valued customer!" "Thank you for past business." "This is our way of thanking you for favors past, present, and future." "Our best regards, and we hope you have a banner year."

Are you getting any guilt pangs as you read this letter? How many times have you loaded your correspondence with this sort of extraneous, useless verbiage?

Okay, that was the "before." Here's the "after"—and the actual letter that went out:

Abe says I'm nuts.

> "Give away radios, stereos? And to customers who are already buying Kleer-Vu products? Why?"

Because I want to induce you to buy more! That's why I created this LUCKY SEVEN-ELEVEN PROMOTION. It's simple, it's

great, it costs you nothing. And look what you get absolutely
FREE:

> You buy 7 items, for a total of $700, and *you get* an
> AM/FM Digital Clock Radio in smart new cube design
> . . . retail value $59.95—FREE.

> You buy 11 items, for a total of $1,100, and *you get* a
> stunning AM/FM Stereo with eight-track stereo car-
> tridge player and matching two-way horn speakers . . .
> retail value $129.95—FREE.

That's all there is to it.

Just look over the enclosed NEW KLEER-VU PRICE LIST which
covers our entire packaged line of Report Covers, Page Protectors, Pencil Cases, Photo Accessories, and our award-winning
Wallet Inserts.

Then pick out seven items totaling $700, eleven items totaling
$1,100 . . . and we'll send your beautiful, valuable prize to you,
or anyone you designate. But do it NOW, because this is a
LIMITED TIME OFFER! Orders must be for delivery before April 15.

Use the handy enclosed order form. Mail it to us, or phone your
order to your Kleer-Vu representative.

> But do it right away, please. I'm anxious to show Abe
> who's really nuts around here.

> > Sincerely yours,

Now that you've read it, can you believe it covers exactly the same points as the "before" letter? Let's see how
it follows my four steps of sales-letter writing:
Step 1: The pull-in. "Abe says I'm nuts." Note the per-

sonal touch that draws the reader into immediate involvement. Why should Abe say "I'm" nuts?

Step 2: Make your point. By the second line the reader knows he can get free radios and stereos. The purpose of the letter and what it offers are immediately apparent.

Step 3: Tell him what he must do to get it. You buy, you get, and see what it's worth. This is the heart of the letter—the pulling-power; thus it is sharply delineated, indented, and set up to stand out.

Step 4: Impel him to do it right now. The limited-time offer, plus the personal plea, ends the letter with a hook couched in a smile.

And notice the immediately stated purpose of the promotion at the beginning of the letter: "Because I want to induce you to buy more." This sets a note of deliberately disarming honesty which adds acceptability to the entire letter.

And the spacing: Note the judicious use of indentation and varied-size paragraphs to make the letter look more alive and inviting.

Now look at the length of the letter. Everything has been accomplished in under half the space of the "before" letter.

Here you have seen an example of how to apply the four-step system to a sales-letter problem. It is merely a matter of organizing what you want to say, into sales-inducing sequence, distilling the message, eschewing the clichés, jettisoning the flowery do-nothing prose, and setting it up in a smart and interesting fashion.

Whenever you are preparing a sales letter, follow the four-step guide, and you really can't miss.

COLORS, PAPER, AND PERSONALIZING

There have been all sorts of direct-mail surveys and studies made on the value of color in sales letters. Red, blue, and black ink on white paper seem to have the edge.

But that's when you're talking about mailing a half million straight-sell letters in a cold call mail-order effort, where every fraction of a cent counts.

My own experience has shown that in small-scale efforts the ink color is just one element in the pulling power of a sales letter. Basically, the letter rises and falls on what it says and how it says it. But of course, it must make an initially appealing, attractive, and readable impression.

A good stock, rag bond or laid finish, is important to give substance and importance. There's nothing that invites instant oblivion faster than an all black-ink letter on shiny cheap sulfite bond. Not only will the letter be ignored, but the company that sent it will be written off as some schlock organization that is hanging in there by nickels and dimes.

The idea of any sales letter is to cleave as closely as possible to the individually typed look. In this computer-crazed era that converts people into numbers everyone welcomes any indication of personalization. Even though you know, deep down, that the letter you receive is but one of thousands, the little delusion that maybe it was prepared especially for you always exists.

That's why a letter should look typewritten, with a signature, and any underscoring or marginal notations printed in blue ink. It's bad enough to know that you're not important enough to warrant a personal letter, but at least you have sufficient standing for the sender to go through the effort of trying to make you think you are. A blatantly mass-printed letter relegates the recipient to a position of total insignificance. It clearly shows the disdain of the sender. And if the sender doesn't care enough to send the very best, why should the reader bother to buy?

The pinnacle of personalization can be achieved by automatic typewriters. These machines individually type letters and stop to insert specific names and addresses—

all automatically. If you have your own automatic editing typewriter in the office, you can easily turn out these wonderfully presentable and effective letters. If not, check around the local letter shops; you're bound to come across one that performs this service.

There are no hard and fast rules for determining the length of a sales letter. Letters that come with appeals for subscriptions to periodicals invariably cover two to four pages. The magazines and book clubs have learned that an in-depth description of what they're offering is necessary to convince an individual to plunk down the money for subscriptions. But remember, these letters are going to homes, where the living is easier, and there's time to sit and study the letter during TV commercials.

If you are selling a product or service that goes to the home—a security system, air conditioning, a pool, a sprinkler system—a long letter is a must.

Tell your story, reiterate the benefits, repeat the construction features, hit away at the economies, stress the conveniences—take all the room you want to convince the prospects that they urgently need your product or service.

Home readers need more persuasion than office readers. The purchasing agent who decides within minutes to issue orders for thousands of dollars of merchandise, equipment, and supplies will agonize for weeks at home over the decision to invest $150 in a lawn mower. Of course, that's *his* money he's spending, which accounts for the intensified caution. Like in a fancy restaurant you can always spot the fellow on an expense account by the cavalier glance he accords the check. But when it's on him, watch the scrutiny and careful tabulating that goes on.

A letter going to places of business is a different bag. Brevity, clarity—just the facts, ma'am. Nobody working at today's frenetic business pace has the time or inclination to mull over mail. Tell it fast, and tell it strongly— get in and out—because the meter is ticking all the while.

Chapter 12

POINT-OF-PURCHASE
DISPLAYS

When you walk into a store, I bet you think it's just a store. Well, it isn't. It's actually a business battlefield you're treading on, with every square inch of floor and counter space fought for ferociously by thousands of manufacturers, wholesalers, and distributors.

This is the final proving ground. It is the point of purchase, where the final truth must be faced: Will the consumer buy your product or service?

The first hurdle has been overcome; you have sold your goods to the wholesale buyer, but only because you've convinced him that your product or service is appealing, valuable, and salable. Now you had better prove it by getting the stuff to move.

The point of purchase is your last push-off point. Everything you have done up to now—advertising, promotion, research, selling—all can be lost unless you catch the elusive eye of the customer and impel him and her to buy *now*.

Of course, once upon a time you could depend on salesclerks to explain and sell. But today most stores are self-service, whether or not they intend to be. The days of the salesmen who care are over. So if you care to move goods, you must join the battle for the floors, walls, counters— and may the best display win.

HOW TO KNOW WHEN YOU NEED A DISPLAY

When one of your salesmen bursts into your office frantically hollering: "Acme just put out a gorgeous floor display and he loaded all my customers with merchandise and I can't write an order to save my life!" then it's too late.

Unfortunately, in small business everyone is too busy just coping with the everyday aggravations of getting the work done, the merchandise shipped, and the bills paid to give thought or time to such exotica as point-of-purchase displays. It's the kind of subject that gets put off "until we get the chance to talk it over." But when the competition hits the field with a display, all of a sudden it's panic time. And the display salesman, who had been trying to make an appointment with the sales manager for five months, is suddenly summoned into emergency session.

What kind of display do they want? Just like the competitor's, of course. Only better, gorgeouser, and cheaper.

A "me too" display will get you nowhere. It makes the company look second best and sell second best. If ever you are forced into that position of counteracting a competitive unit, at least make yours different. There are many approaches to every display situation. Avoid the temptation to imitate.

But why allow yourself to get put into that bind? The time to think about a display is now.

SITUATIONS THAT SCREAM FOR DISPLAYS

Selling a product to a buyer is hard. Selling a selling unit is easier. When you come into a new market and want to introduce your line, offer it in a display unit. The buyer will be more willing to take a chance on an item that you have packaged to sell itself.

No store salesman is going to stand around and explain the virtues of your new product, no matter how great and unique. If you don't inform the consuming public of its existence and tell them the marvelous things it can achieve for them, your new creation will remain unsung, undiscovered, and unsold. You must accompany every new product with some sort of point-of-purchase education device—some means of telling the selling story.

If you have the kind of product that is stocked away on shelves, awaiting requests from the purchaser who is lucky enough to find a salesperson who will reach for it, getting the stuff onto the selling floor can change your entire sales picture. A display can make your merchandise visible and accessible to the brouser and buyer.

Every dealer has his favorites—the items in your line that he has been buying for years. It's hard to get him interested in the many other good or different numbers you make. He's loath to get involved in new stock numbers, new inventory, new anything. The status quo is so comfortable, why rock the selling boat? Here's where a display can do the job. Create a unit that carries an in-depth selection of your products, and you make it easy for him to expand his purchases—and sales—of your merchandise.

It's Mother's Day, graduation, or spring cleanup time— or just a two-for-one offer. A special promotion must have a special display to remind the store personnel as well as the customers.

HOW TO DECIDE WHAT KIND OF DISPLAY TO USE

First off, you must case the field you plan to hit. In what kind of market will the display appear? Mass merchandisers, supermarkets, novelty stores, drugstores, specialty stores, Mom-and-Pop stores, wholesalers' showrooms, gas stations, beauty shops—wherever.

Each market has its own particular set of specifications, and if you don't conform, you're dead. For no matter how stunning—even if it walks, sings, and talks—if it's the wrong dimensions or the wrong type of unit, it will never reach the selling floor.

There are four ways to find out the special display demands of an industry and to evolve the best kind of unit in which your merchandise should be presented to that field.

1. Trade associations. Every industry has its trade association. Contact them and tell them your problem. They can provide invaluable information about the design limitations and specifications of the industry, if there are any. Some of the larger ones will supply you with printed material that establishes display guidelines.

2. Your salesmen. Talk to your men in the field. Or if you're planning to enter a new field, talk with the sales representatives you intend to engage. Find out what sort of displays are around, which they have noticed are more effective, and what the competition is doing.

3. Trade magazines. Take a space salesman to lunch. He is a walking encyclopedia of promotional advice.

4. Hit the road yourself. This is the big "must." Get out and get around, to small stores, big stores, in urban areas and suburban areas and small towns. Look around, inspect, chat with the dealers and store personnel. Just don't open by asking a direct question like "What kind of display do you think we ought to make?" Or you'll get that blank look that masks the cranial confusion most people experience when confronted with a question that requires a creative opinion. Or you may be subjected to a dogmatic discourse by some self-appointed retailing expert who

never allows his ignorance to deter him from giving assertive advice.

Just ease your way around, examine the store displays, and ask opinions of the value of the various types you see. Find out which kind sells, which kind the store manager likes and why. And notice the position awarded each display unit, and analyze why one kind gets better billing than another.

After you have completed your research, you will have formulated some ideas as to the kind of display unit that would work best in your market—for your type of product—for your specific promotional need.

TYPES OF DISPLAYS AVAILABLE

The cigar-store Indian, the barber pole, the pawn broker's ball trio—these are all point-of-purchase displays. Anything that creates interest and moves goods at the point of sale is, by definition, a point-of-purchase display.

There are five main types of displays: signs (indoor, outdoor, clocks, decals), counter displays, floor units, wall-hung displays, and ceiling-hung displays. They can be made of any of the following materials, listed according to cost, starting with the least expensive.

1. Cardboard
2. Corrugated
3. Wire
4. Masonite
5. Sheet Metal
6. Wood
7. Plastic

Each type of material lends itself to different situations. Now let's go into the many ways and whys of using the various fabricating elements available.

Cardboard and Corrugated—The Cheapies

A mounted reprint of an advertisement is the simplest and cheapest display possible. If you have run a consumer ad, you can have the magazine run off extra copies and mount them for you. This is effective at the point of purchase because it reminds buyers who may have seen the ad that "oh, yes—that's the gizmo I wanted to see."

Or if you have printed a selling sheet that's attractive, simple (not garbaged up with paragraphs of small type and dealer terminology), and *consumer-oriented*, you could have it mounted and easeled into a display. Frankly, I hesitate to even suggest this, because I have seen too many purely industrial catalog sheets that have been mounted, sent out, and thrown out. It's a terrible temptation, I agree, to try to amortize the expense of the printing and preparation of a dealer catalog sheet by deluding yourself into thinking it can perform double duty.

"It shows the product, it tells the price—what more does a display need?" Plenty. It needs a reason for the consumers to buy. It needs applications that are recognizable to them. It needs big pictures, big type, and a design that should be visible from across the store.

You can prepare a catalog sheet with that double use in mind and save money, but you must plan for it beforehand. For instance, we made a catalog sheet to introduce a new lamp for the student market. One side was totally consumer-oriented, with a series of photos showing the lamp being used in student-type situations. The other side had dealer information—packing, discount, colors, etc. The dealer got the two-sided sheet. The consumer side suggested to him why the lamp would be bought and how his store personnel could pitch it. For consumer display use we printed a few thousand one-side-only and had them mounted.

Or you might design a special counter card. Perhaps you have a one-cent sale offer or a two-for-one deal or a special-time-of-the-year bargain. Then it pays to have a counter card made up for the occasion. But only if it is for limited-time-only use. Because displays are highly expendable, and number one on the discard list is the counter card.

This sort of display could also be made of vacuum-formed plastic, which is feasible in quantities of two to three thousand. It could be used to display the product, such as having a niche in which the product fits. So the sign becomes part of an effective demonstrator display for counter or window.

If you're lucky enough to have a tiny product that can be mounted en masse on a card (razor blades, batteries, flints, etc.), you can use a counter card as a dispenser display.

The small display cards that are clipped on the ends of supermarket shelves are known as shelf-talkers. They're good for limited specials, since they will be kept around for short terms only.

You see self-shippers everywhere, everyday. These are the shipping cartons that convert into counter (or sometimes floor) displays. A few dozen assorted to the box. Dealer opens box, folds cover in half, thereby exposing printed display material, tucks it into the back of the box, and—*poof!*—it's a display, filled with merchandise and ready to sell.

It's about the simplest, least expensive way to create a self-service display. This is ideal for small merchandise assortments on a counter. For large, heavier products, the same concept can be used with a corrugated floor unit. This is called a dump display and is quite popular with mass merchandisers. Just be sure to check size specifications here. The supermarkets, who are big users of dump displays, will not accept anything over waist height (twenty-four to thirty-six inches square is the popular size), and the sign that stands up in back must be no taller than sixty inches.

Of course, you realize that self-shippers are self-disposables. When the merchandise is finished, so is the display. On the plus side you avoid the follow-up problem of keeping the display stocked. But on the other hand, it's a one-shot deal, which means the cost of the display must be paid for out of the profit on the contained merchandise. You can't amortize the unit from future business that comes from refilling, as with permanent displays.

Wire—Efficiency without Elegance

Sometimes display-suppliers get fancy and call these wrought iron, but they're just plain bent wire. A wire display is about the cheapest permanent unit you can get, although it doesn't have to look it. A smartly designed sign and brightly colored wire (it has to be dipped to make it black anyway, so why not use blue, yellow, or red instead?) can make the unit reasonably attractive.

They fold nice and flat, are easy to ship, and are a snap to set up (which is an important factor). They can be made counter size, floor style, or wall style to fit on a pegboard.

Wire displays are inoffensive and functional, but they have no class. So if you are selling high-ticket stuff, wire is not the way to go.

Wood, Masonite, Metal, and Plastic— The Quality Look

Now we're getting into the top-drawer department— the displays that convey high-level quality, value, and style and of course, carry a high-level price tag.

A wooden display can cost anywhere from fifteen to

one hundred dollars. I've seen manufacturers pale visibly at the suggestion of giving away such expensive units to their dealers. "Why the hell should I pay for furnishing the dealer's store? It's his fixture—why shouldn't he pay for it?"

There are a few answers to that oft-heard plaintive plea. First, he doesn't *have* to pay for it. There are hundreds of guys just pleading to give him displays. Second, you are not furnishing his store. In fact, you are not giving him anything—*he* is giving *you*. You are, in effect, leasing space in his store to sell your product. It's strictly a real-estate transaction, and he's in the seller's seat. Third, there are painless ways of splitting the cost with the dealer that can work out quite nicely. We'll get to that shortly.

The basic display used in all self-service stores today is called the gondola. I don't know what romantic soul applied a name that conjures up soft images of sailing along under moonlight to a bulky unit that stands and sells under fluorescents. The gondola fixture ranges in height from fifty-four to sixty inches, widths of thirty-six, forty-eight, and sixty inches, is sheathed in pegboard, comes with standards and shelves, and is finished off at the bottom with a kick base.

A variation of this unit is your best bet, since it is most readily adaptable to all retail outlets. And remember, that's the important consideration.

A floor-display unit is an investment. It should be used to create a complete self-service selling center for your merchandise, where a consumer can see, pick, and choose the exact version he or she needs. It is the best way to get your products onto the selling floor in a more conspicuous, heavily trafficked location.

And it's forever. It's permanent and can produce sales for years to come. Here are some typical case histories of how a fixture-type unit revolutionized companies' sales.

(Examples courtesy of Krebs Merchandising Displays Corporation, 619 West 56th Street, New York, N. Y. 10019.)

Case History #1: Hohner Harmonica is a respected, established company that has been manufacturing harmonicas for over 115 years. Almost every music store carried some representation of Hohner instruments, but few carried the complete line. The problem was how to get each dealer to expand his Hohner purchases and carry the line in depth. The solution was a self-contained Hohner harmonica center—a handsome wooden fixture that showed a sample of every style Hohner harmonica and contained backup stock within. It was made forty inches high to fit so that it would line up with regulation music-store counters. Results: The music stores found they were turning over Hohner harmonicas five times faster than ever before and selling new instruments they had never before handled. Letters came in to ad manager Gil Matthies from dealers with praise and statements like "Never knew you had such a wide variety of harmonicas."

When you realize that the music-store buyers have been reading the Hohner catalogs for years and were still unaware of the extent of the Hohner line, you get some idea of the degree of dedication and depth of concentration you can expect from dealers. And that accounts for the frequency with which a store clerk will answer your query for a particular product with the flat surly statement "They don't make that." Which translated means, "I never heard of it."

This points up the secondary benefit of a full-line display: It educates the store personnel. It makes them aware of the many styles and variations available, so that even when temporarily out of stock, at least they'll know enough to say, "We can order it for you," instead of "They don't make it."

Case History #2: Bassick makes various casters and

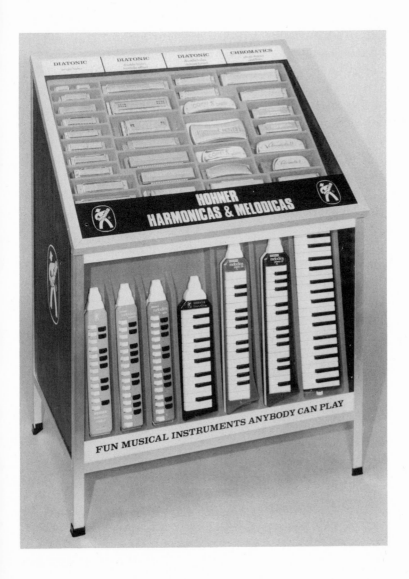

glides that are carded and sold in hardware stores. As you know, hardware stores carry thousands of small items, and Bassick found that their merchandise was being relegated to haphazard positions on the stores' pegboard setups. A customer who came in for casters really had to search, and a shopper who came in for something else and could have been reminded to buy casters, if he had seen them, was a total loss.

The cure was to take the casters out of hiding by creating a buying center. A gondola unit was built that conformed to the parameters of hardware-retailers and contained a good varied assortment of easily identifiable merchandise. Result: of course, a tremendous increase in sales.

The same approach can be used for any product. If your display turns over merchandise at a good rate, the retailer will accept it. He doesn't care what kind of unit takes up his valuable floor space as long as it moves merchandise and produces the prescribed amount of profit per inch.

And the same principle applies to counter units. If your product or budget doesn't warrant a floor unit, a counter unit can do a good job. This, too, can be self-contained with display samples in front and storaged stock behind. The depth of the counter unit is no problem, since nothing else can go behind it. Counter space is allotted on a width basis only, so the narrower, the better.

THE NO-RISK WAY OF BUYING DISPLAYS

The one thing you don't want to do is order two hundred displays and then find out that nobody wants them. There are prescribed ways of hedging your bet and avoiding the risk of the unknown, of ascertaining the acceptability of the display beforehand, of knowing in advance how many display units you will be able to sell.

When you have decided conclusively that you need and want a display, here is the procedure to follow.

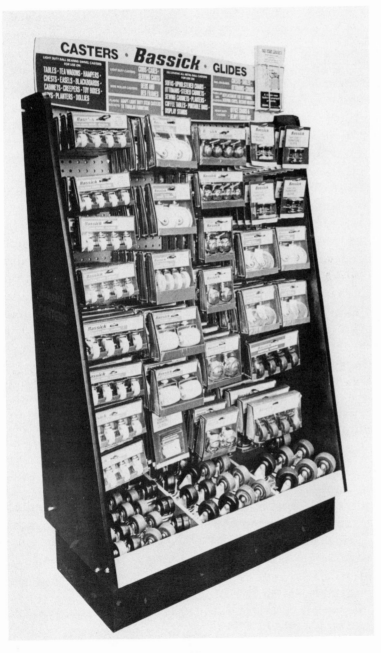

Select a point-of-purchase supplier. There are hundreds and hundreds of companies who design and produce displays. Select a few, and call them in to discuss your specific problem. When you have arrived at the one you feel is most experienced, helpful, and creative, ask them to submit a few sketches.

Show sketches to selected big buyers. There's nothing more flattering than to be placed in the role of respected expert, and that's the position in which you place a buyer when you ask his or her opinions on the value of your projected display. Their advice and suggestions can be an invaluable contribution. After all, they deal with displays constantly and are fully familiar with what's good, bad, and needed. And you're in good shape from a future selling point of view, too, because their involvement in the creation of the display almost insures their ultimate purchase of it.

Have a prototype made. The display company will set a price on the manufacture of a single prototype which covers their costs fairly. The usual practice is to credit that charge toward your order. In other words, if you do not go ahead with the production, you pay for the sample unit. If you do go into production, the sample is free.

Have photographs of the prototype made. Show the actual prototype at trade shows, furnish photographs of it to salesmen, send out mailings on it, and write up orders with a promise of a few months' delivery. You will then be in the lovely safe position of knowing exactly how many displays to buy and in no danger of being stuck with a warehouse full of unwanted displays.

"How much can we afford to spend on a display?" is a frequently asked question, and there's a variety of answers. The rule of thumb is 10 percent of the total net cost of the initial deal that goes along with the unit. In other words, you give away ten dollars for every one hundred dollars' worth of goods purchased.

However, what you really should ask is how can you afford not to spend on a display. A permanent display unit is an investment. It is an annuity that will continue to produce income. As to who carries the expenditure, it is customarily chalked up to the advertising department or the sales department of your company, depending upon who loses the fight.

THE NO-COST WAY OF BUYING DISPLAYS

There is a juggling money technique that works quite well with display deals and ends up with neither you nor the dealer paying for the unit. That's what it seems like, but it's like a shell game. Actually, it's the dealer who pays, but in such a psychologically effective way that it doesn't hurt a bit.

Here's how it works. Say the display has cost you $15. This is how you present it to the dealers.

NEW INTRODUCTORY DISPLAY DEAL

You buy . . . $150 net worth of merchandise.
You pay . . . $ 20 for the display.
You get free . . . $ 20 *retail* worth of merchandise
                         to cover your cost of the
                         display.

After you have sold the $20 worth of goods, you have made the cost of the unit; thus the display costs you nothing.

To the dealer, it looks like fancy bookkeeping, where on the one hand you charge for the display, and on the other hand you give him the means for making the money to pay for it.

For you, the display is totally free. The economics are like this: The free merchandise (that retails for $20) costs you around $5, right? The display costs you $15. The dealer has paid you $20. Thus the display costs you $0!

It's a lovely arrangement and one that is used by many companies very successfully. Of course, there's a fallacy. The $20 retail worth of merchandise normally costs the dealer $10, or whatever his discount brings it down to. So you are really giving him $10, not $20. Which means he is paying for the display. But it doesn't feel like it, because he doesn't have to put out a dime—and psychologically, that feels like free.

PROMOTE YOUR P.O.P.

It's new, it's great—it's the hottest thing to hit selling floors since pipe racks. That's the story you want to get across—and *quick*.

Send out mailings, feature the deal in trade ads, but blanket the field fast. This has to be engineered and planned like you're General Patton, with surprise and speed as your prime strategy. Because once your competition gets wind of the display that threatens to displace and overshadow their line, you can bet that they're not going to sit on their duffs and watch you move in.

So before they can marshal their forces and come up kicking, clawing, and fighting with deals, offers, and other retaliatory razzle-dazzle, you had better be sure you have saturated the field and have achieved complete coverage.

While the display is still in the design stage, you can prepare your promotion plans. You might consider "spiffs" for your sales force—a bonus for each display sold. Or sales contests among them, with maybe a premium gift for each six sold and a top prize for the one who sells the most.

Develop a six-month program; keep it lively, and keep it moving. Your aim is to maintain a high pitch of interest and enthusiasm among your salespeople and customers. After all, no matter how great a display is, it won't produce a nickel unless you get it out into the performing arena. So talk it up.

HOW TO BE SURE YOUR DISPLAY
KEEPS ON SELLING

Lights, Action

To shed light on your merchandise is lovely. Built-in lighting can be a plus factor for your display if you are selling to dealers in downtown areas. They can then use the display as a night-light, and you have the advantage of your name in lights twenty-four hours a day, visible to all passersby. However, the era of downtown business is ebbing. And the pleasures of evening strolling have been destroyed by fear. An electrified display requires proximity to an outlet, which poses a problem of positioning in the store. And then, you run into the chintzy retailer who complains about the costly juice being consumed. So all in all, electricity is a needless expense.

Action and motion are great attention-getters, albeit a bit costly. Jumping figures, rotating products, and other movements can be achieved with electricity, but then you have the problems mentioned before. Battery-operated motors are available at fairly low cost, well under one dollar each. But you must accept the reality that when the battery dies, so does the display. No dealer will bother to replace a battery.

No Dogs Allowed

One slow mover can kill an entire display. I know it's tempting to try to pass off a few "dogs" when arranging an assortment—sort of a tie-in package forcing the dealer to take the bad with the good. But it can destroy the effectiveness of the unit, and the only one penalized is you. A good display contains a balanced assortment with quantities of each item determined by its popularity. Twelve of the fast movers to one of the slow numbers, or whatever is a realistic appraisal of their sales-moving potential. In theory the perfect display assortment empties from the shelves in unison.

Don't Let Ego Reign

The suggestion may arise in the executive office to throw a sample of everything the company makes into a display. It may do big things for the boss's ego to show the world what a grand, big line he produces, but it will do very small things for sales. Arrange your assortment fairly. Put in only what you know the dealer can move in his particular marketing arena. The determining factor is sales, not ego.

The Rule Is Realism

If you're working with a modest volume field, like small specialty stores, what's the point of setting up a display deal that requires an initial order of seven hundred dollars? You'll only scare off the little guys and cancel your cause. Sure it would be nice to make up the entire cost of the display the first time around, but reality must rule, or the display will never get out to work for you. Evaluate the dollar amount that is acceptable to the market you are aiming for, and set up your merchandise deal accordingly. Be patient; you will make up the cost in time as the display produces sales for years and years.

Pilfer-Proof Means Sales-Proof

The buyer wants your display to be pilfer-proof and asks you to package the product so that it is inaccessible. He also would like you to figure out a way to protect the product from the ravages of customer handling. But in the next breath the buyer tells you that the merchandise had better sell. So where are you? If you close off the products so that they're unattainable and seal them in so that they're untouchable, how will people buy them?

One idea is to have samples on display and boxed stock below. But don't bank on this method as the solution. Customers have been known to open boxes to examine the product and then insist on a fresh clean unhandled one. So the answer is, don't worry. Your prime aim is to sell. Put the stuff where everyone can get to it, and let the store managers worry about pilferage and handling.

No Riders Allowed

It hurts to see competitive merchandise on your display. Yet it's a natural procedure for the dealer to put similar items together and a common tactic of competitors to try to hitch a free ride on your unit.

Some of this is inevitable, and you may take some comfort in the fact that your name appears on the unit and the predominant proportion of contents will always be yours. But sometimes you can cut down on this competitive incursion by designing the display in such a way as to accommodate your goods only.

For instance, if you have packaged your products in a unique shape, it's easy to have hooks that support only that shape. Or perhaps your boxes vary in dimensions. Build the shelves to accommodate your sizes only.

As I said, some infringement is inevitable. But by considering this problem beforehand and making a pointed effort to tailor your display and make it unsuitable for anyone else's merchandise, you can cut down on free riders somewhat.

Keep It Clean; Keep It Filled

What's more dreary looking than a half-empty, dusty display? Or more aggravating than seeing empty useless shelf space that could be functionally featuring and selling your goods? Servicing displays is a problem, and you must keep on top of it with periodic prodding.

Keep nudging your salesmen to visit every store to which they've sold a display. Urge them to see that it's tidy and filled. Point out that the display works for them while they are not there. But the only way to get the full profit benefit of this nice steady business-builder is to keep replenishing the merchandise that's moved. Give them a proprietary feeling about each unit they place; make them realize that they have a vested interest in maintaining these "assistant salesmen."

Keep a record of every store who has a display, and send periodic reminders and order forms to the store managers. Maybe some sort of incentive—a special personal gift to the manager or an extra discount refill deal.

The main point to remember is that placing the displays on the dealers' floors is not the end of your or the salesmen's responsibility—it's only the beginning.

CHAPTER 13

SELECTING AN ADVERTISING AGENCY

When you place an ad, you as the advertiser are billed at the regular publication rate. If you have an agency place the ad, you still pay that rate—only the agency gets a 15 percent commission from the publication.

So it costs you nothing. And you get the benefit of professional creativity and guidance. And someone to handle the traffic of ordering space and checking insertions and seeing that the artwork is sent off in time—and all the headaches involved thereof.

That doesn't mean you get the preparation of the ad free. But you would pay for that in any event (even if you went to the publication and had their limited art and copy department turn it out).

The usual practice is that an agency will not charge you for layout and copy for an ad if the ad will bring sufficient revenue from the 15 percent commission to cover their labors.

For instance, if you are running a half-page ad in *The*

Chronicle of the Horse magazine, which costs a big $145, you can't expect to get well-planned art and copy free when the agency will get $21.75 income. The clerical time and postage involved in mailing insertion orders would blow their whole profit. However, if your ad will yield anywhere over $150 commission, then copy and layout should be provided at no charge.

You will be billed for the labor of producing the ad— the mechanical and production. And all elements purchased by them for inclusion in the ad, such as typography, photographs, and photostats, are billed to you with a markup.

Twenty percent is the current markup figure you pay for an agency's buying services. Whatever they buy for you, the 20 percent is added to their purchase price. This covers their handling, ordering, billing, banking, and supervising. And that last item can be mighty important, especially in printing.

You can have the agency create a mailing piece for you and hand the camera-ready finished mechanical over to you. And you can arrange to have it printed yourself, work directly with the printer, and save the 20 percent markup. Just be fully aware of the risk and responsibility.

For instance, can you read a blueprint (or Vandyke)? We checked the blueprint proof on a large printing job recently and immediately spotted that the printer had made the error of putting solid color over the main product photo. That would have resulted in fifty thousand folders featuring a lovely bright-red heavy-duty electric carbonator. Now this may seem like the sort of flagrant mistake that's easy to pick up. But remember, a blueprint is prepared in one color; only gradations of blue distinguish what will be black from what will ultimately appear in color. And you need a trained eye to spot that sort of subtlety. As a matter of fact, the client sent the blueprint back to us with his signed okay, having completely missed that color overprint.

It's a markup well worth paying. And I'm not saying that because I am in the agency business. After all, you can do your own contracting when building a house or finishing a basement. You can shop for your own materials, search and find the right carpenter, electrician, painter, and you can work with them to coordinate their comings and goings to dovetail properly. You can wheedle when they welsh and plead when they procrastinate. You most certainly will save the contractor's markup, but you'd better have a lot of time to spare and a wholesale source for Gelusil.

An ad agency takes the entire production process off your hands and insures that everything is done right. So pay the two dollars—it's worth it.

HOW TO SELECT YOUR AD AGENCY

Now that you know all about advertising, sales promotion, merchandising, and marketing and know how much you can and want to do yourself, it's time to consider the possibilities of hiring an ad agency to help out.

There are probably a number of agencies in your area to choose from, but there's one unique aspect of your account that determines which type of shop to approach: The budget is a limited one. You are a special kind of business that requires a specific kind of attention and expertise.

Small-Fish-in-a-Big-Pond Possibility

From time to time when their billing gets shaky, large agencies will scramble for small accounts to tide them over the dollar crisis. They are driven by desperation, and that's just the kind of service you will get—desperate.

Large-agency operations are just not geared to the demands of small-budget clients. They have no understanding of the merchandising and marketing problems of small business. They have no concept of dealer thinking, since consumers are their sole goal. They may do great things with full-page ads in *Sports Illustrated,* but a half page in *Administrative Management* is just not their cup of gin. And since the high-priced hotshots in their creative stable would scorn to employ their collective genius on trade-magazine stuff—and the agency couldn't afford to put them on low-yield media ads—your account is immediately sloughed off to the new kid.

The pitch to get your account may be the last attempt at concerned creativity you get. Because in their shop you are small potatoes and a big nuisance. You may like the sound of saying that your ad agency is someone like J. Walter Thompson, but the benefit stops there.

There are three basic categories of small agencies. Like the Three Bears, one is disastrous, one is functional, and one is just right. These brief rundowns should help you to distinguish one from the other and protect you from falling into the wrong shop for you.

The Stepping-stone Operation

The stepping-stone operation is the agency run by young, hot, ambitious guys who are on the make for the big time. These boys regard small accounts as really no accounts, but merely as stepping stones to be used temporarily until the real thing comes along.

They are out to win attention, win awards, make a big splash in the current ad scene. As a result, the work they prepare for you is calculated to be smart-looking, with-it —the sort of ads that sell them but rarely you. They'll try to talk you into handsome, flashy four-color ads instead of the possibly more constructive and sales-producing program of half-page black-and-white ads. They'll push for TV spots that may take a half year's budget. They think big, for them. They are out to build a portfolio, not your business.

It's easy to be captivated by this sort of group. They're usually enthusiastic, talented, and winning. And I wish them all the luck in the world. It's nice to see them get ahead—just be sure it's not on your back.

The Sausage-Style Agency

Years ago, when I started in this so-called ad game, I worked for a small agency where ads and direct mail were ground out like sausages. There was a set recipe, standard ingredients, and an assembly-line production. The only things missing were taste and quality control.

All ads looked basically alike. At some early point in his career, the agency principal had achieved good results for a client with an ad that had a reverse headline and reverse logo at the bottom. That became his distinctive if not distinguished design formula. After all, why fight success, even if it did happen ten years ago. The headings ranged from "Impulse buy-item!" to "Fast turnover—big profits!" (always with the exclamation points—he was very big on those). You picked one from Group A or one from Group B. Who had time for creativity? The economics of the operation wouldn't allow it. If by chance, someone happened to hit on a thrilling new caption like "Save and sell!" (note the impressive alliteration) it would become that month's heading.

The ads were functional, and that was about it. Many clients found the work completely satisfactory, and if they learned better or needed more, they left. But since the agency serviced a slew of small accounts, nobody missed the defector, and another callow client was sure to come along eventually anyhow.

This sort of small-agency operation exists today. In fact, it is quite common. Prices are low, volume is high, but creativity is nil. If that's all you need, fine.

Perhaps you only require someone to turn out specification sheets, price lists, fast buckeye flyers, daily special sheets—the sort of material where only neatness counts. Maybe you just need someone to handle the mechanics of your printing output. Then this sausage-style agency is quite adequate. Why pay for creativity you will never need?

The Pro Principal Agency

And last we have the sort of small personalized operation headed by one or two pros, experienced creative professionals who work on each account themselves. Your problems are not passed on to juniors. By nature, this style shop will handle only a limited number of clients because each gets the benefit of the principals' individual attention.

You may pay more for their work but usually not much more, if at all. Because the pro principal agency is not burdened with the big staff demanded by the volume of twenty to fifty accounts serviced by the sausage shops. In other words you are paying for creativity, not overhead.

This sort of organization will work closely with you and familiarize themselves with your marketing, manufacturing, and sales situations. They aim to build a permanent relationship with their client and to ultimately function as your marketing and sales-promotion arm. Over the years of working with companies of comparable size, they have encountered similar situations, have handled parallel sales, advertising and marketing problems, and can offer you a tremendous source of experience and commercial wisdom.

WHAT'S BEST FOR YOU

Before you embark on a search for an agency, decide which kind will be best for your needs. Then start interviewing, and be sure to establish which category each falls into. Ask to see samples of work done for other accounts. If you spot a sameness of style, a similarity in copy, design, and concepts among the accounts, chances are it's the sausage shop. If their portfolio is way out and arty, most likely you have encountered a stepping-stone type.

Look for the series approach as opposed to the one-shot ads—that's a distinct indication of an agency's quality of work. The good agency will create a total approach concept to a client's advertising and will design a series of ads that have a theme and pervasive design relationship. This establishes a recognition factor that increases the readers' subliminal association from one ad to the other.

The sausage shop usually knocks out ads shot for shot. The hours involved in agonizing over a theme are not stock items listed on their time sheets. Each ad is turned out as it's needed. It looks like other ads, yes, but not necessarily yours.

It's like the discount chain versus the neighborhood store. When you know exactly what you want, the discount store is fine. But Lord help you if you need some advice on distinctions between products or information on available variations. The Lord had better help you, because no one else will. Then you need a local store with a knowledgeable, concerned proprietor who gives a damn. You may pay a bit more, but you're ultimately saving money by getting the right product to suit your exact needs.

As you can undoubtedly tell, I strongly favor the pro principal style. I have worked in and with all three kinds and know exactly what services and benefits each type provides. There's just no contest in comparable value offered.

When I worked in the sausage shop, I saw how the client's needs were subordinated to the agency's needs. The prime aim was to produce a profit for the agency; the client's profit picture was strictly secondary. If the agency could make more money from a specific type of mailing—for example, if the boss could get a good price from running three catalog sheets together—then that was the kind of mailing he pushed to the clients. Whether or not it would be the most effective sort of literature for them was not important. The thought was, it couldn't hurt.

It reminds me of a discussion I had with the owner of an automobile-repair shop. When I brought up the hit-or-miss type of car repairs performed by most mechanics, he agreed with this comforting rationale: "When in doubt, we replace the whole system. So maybe the guy doesn't really need it now. But he's bound to someday, isn't he? So it can't hurt."

This "it can't hurt" school of advertising is no way to decide which way to go. It has to help sales actively, or it isn't worth doing.

The pro principal agency has to think of the account first, if for no other reason than the selfish one of keeping the client. The sausage style tries to make as much from each job as they can, since they work on a here-today basis, because they know that the client is often gone tomorrow.

The smaller personalized style of the pro principal agency means you will have someone working for you whose interests coincide directly with yours. They want to produce sales for you; they want your company to grow; they want to provide the best possible advertising and marketing service in order to build a lasting relationship. Because that's what their business depends on.

We have accounts for whom we have decorated new offices, designed housing for new equipment, hired sales representatives, written and produced annual reports. Because over the years of association they have come to depend on us to handle all problems involving creativity, marketing, and sales. It is a dependency that has been fostered by our ability and willingness to fulfill all these needs.

This is the sort of one-stop-shopping service needed by every small business. It can be an invaluable asset in your day-by-day activities and an immeasurable contribution toward the future growth of your company.

INDEX